Kids' Pumpkin Projects

A WILLIAMSON *GOOD TIMES!* **BOOK**

Little Hands®, *Kids Can!*®, and *Tales Alive!*® are registered trade-
marks of Williamson Publishing Company.
Kaleidoscope Kids™ is a trademark of Williamson Publishing Company.

**LIBRARY OF CONGRESS
CATALOGING-IN-PUBLICATION DATA**

Cook, Deanna F., 1965-
  Kids' pumpkin projects: planting & harvest fun
  / Deanna F. Cook.
      p. cm.
    Summary: Provides instruction for projects and activities
    involving pumpkins, including growing them, using them in
    recipes, and making things out of them.
    ISBN 1-885593-21-X
    1. Handicraft—Juvenile literature. 2. Cookery (Pumpkin)
  Juvenile literature. 3. Pumpkin—Juvenile literature.
  [1. Pumpkin. 2. Cookery—Pumpkin. 3. Handicraft.]   I. Title.
    TT160.C667   1998
    745.5—dc21   97-48366
                                                         CIP
                                                          AC

CREDITS
COVER DESIGN: Trezzo-Braren Studio
ILLUSTRATIONS: Kate Flanagan
INTERIOR DESIGN: Foxwater Design
PRINTING: Capital City Press

WILLIAMSON PUBLISHING CO.
P.O. BOX 185
CHARLOTTE, VERMONT 05445
800-234-8791

Manufactured in the United States of America

10 9 8 7 6 5 4 3 2 1

Dedication

For my daughter, Ella

ACKNOWLEDGEMENTS

Special thanks to the students in Kristen
Roeder's class at the Hilltown Cooperative
Charter School in Haydenville, Massachusetts,
and the kids who tended the pumpkin patch
in my Northampton, Massachusetts,
neighborhood. I'd also like to thank Gordon
Pullan for helping me write the pumpkin
poem and Cindy Littlefield for her Native
American pumpkin facts and activities.
Also, thanks to songwriter Ed Kohn for writing
"The Pumpkin Seed Song" on page 23.
Special thanks to Emily Stetson and Susan
Williamson for pulling this pumpkin book
together. Finally, without the support of my
husband, Doug, this book would have
just been a pumpkin dream.

A WILLIAMSON *GOOD TIMES!* BOOK

Kids' Pumpkin Projects

Planting & Harvest Fun

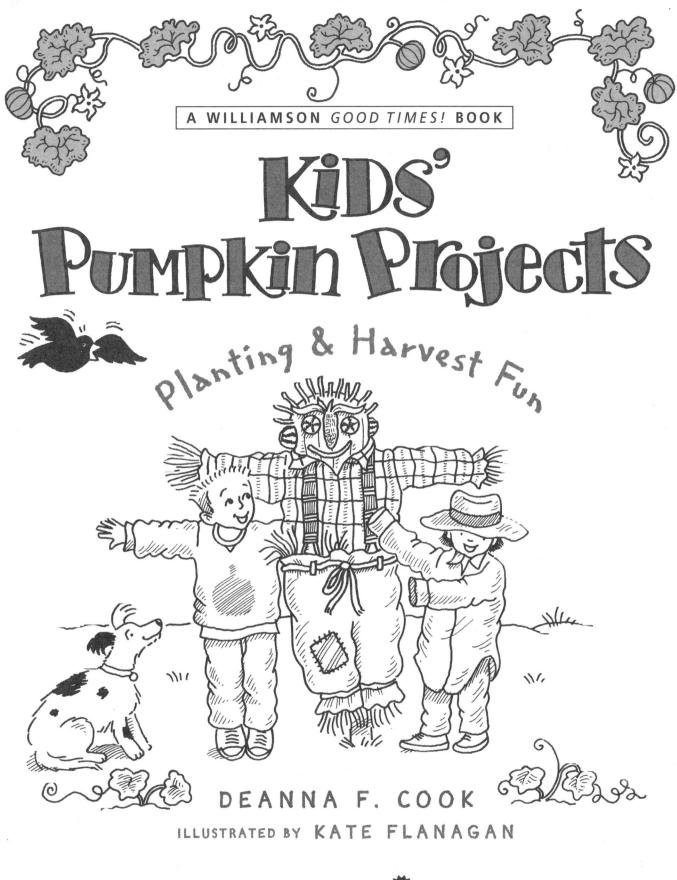

DEANNA F. COOK

ILLUSTRATED BY KATE FLANAGAN

WILLIAMSON PUBLISHING COMPANY CHARLOTTE, VT 05445

c o n t e n t s

FALL
Pumpkin Harvest, Celebrations, Lore . . . and Pie!   53

WINTER
Bedtime for the Pumpkin Patch, Saving Seeds, and Pumpkin Tales, Food, and Crafts   79

introduction

My grandmother always said, "The best pumpkin pie starts in the garden." Every Thanksgiving, she made pumpkin pie from a real pumpkin—one that she had planted early in the spring in her backyard. That's the way the Pilgrims did it, and that's the way my Grandma Cook did it, too.

This past summer, I asked the kids in my Massachusetts neighborhood, "Where does pumpkin pie come from?" A few thought it came from a can of pumpkin that you buy in the grocery store and put in a piecrust. So together, we set out to make pumpkin pie from scratch. And guess what—it didn't start in a can at all! It began in a small corner of a garden.

Eight neighborhood kids helped me order pumpkin seeds in the early spring, plant them in the early summer, and turn them into pie in the fall. Along the way, we crafted pumpkin planting T-shirts, drew pictures of the sprawling vines, discussed pumpkin lore and Native American traditions, and learned basic gardening skills—watering, weeding, fertilizing, and mulching. In the late October, after our harvest, we had a pumpkin carnival, complete with pumpkin games and jack-o'-lantern carving. Best of all, we baked homemade pumpkin pies from scratch. No cans for us!

Like my grandmother, we now know where the best pumpkin pie (and a host of other pumpkin-inspired foods) comes from, and we know a lot more about pumpkin lore and Native American gardening as well. Follow the growing vine to embark on *your* journey through the pumpkin patch.

SPRING

Pumpkin Dreams, Plans, Plots, and Planting

Growing a pumpkin garden is fun and easy to do. It is part dreaming, part math, part getting your hands dirty, and part celebration. In the early spring, you get to do the dreaming, deciding what you want to grow. Are you hoping to have one giant pumpkin, harvest a pack of pie- and carving-sized globes (maybe even a ghostly white variety), or celebrate in fall with dozens of mini-pumpkins? Maybe you'll grow beans, corn, and pumpkins in a Native American–style garden. It's up to you.

While the weather is still too wet or cold outside for planting, decide what you want your pumpkin plot to look like (do your dreaming). Then, plan and plot it out on paper (that's the math). Once you know what you want (and what will fit), you can order or buy seeds and prepare the soil. That's the getting-your-hands-dirty part. As soon as the weather is warm enough, you'll be ready to plant — and celebrate!

When winter is almost over,
And squishy mud covers the yard,
Start your pumpkin journal
And dream of the garden to come.

Start a Pumpkin Journal!

A pumpkin journal is a great way to keep track of everything that happens on your journey through the pumpkin patch. It is where you plan, draw, graph, and write about your pumpkin garden. You'll find ideas in this book to guide you in your journaling, but don't stop there! Take pictures of your garden with a camera and glue them into the pages of your journal. Tape in seeds, flowers, and leaves from your plants. Track the weather. Chart your garden's growth. Paint a pumpkin picture. Make up a pumpkin riddle. Tell a pumpkin tale. When you've harvested the last pumpkin and your pie is all gone, you'll have this pumpkin keepsake to look back on and share with your family and friends . . . and use to plan *next* year's pumpkin plot!

What you need:

2 sheets construction paper (for the front and back covers) ◆ 20 to 30 sheets of white paper ◆ Stapler, or a paper punch and brass fasteners, ribbon, or twine ◆ Markers, pencils, watercolors, and other art supplies

What you do:

1 Decorate one piece of construction paper for the front cover of your pumpkin journal. You can cut a big pumpkin out of orange paper and glue it onto the cover. Or, draw a pumpkin on white paper with orange markers.

2 Give your journal a title, such as *[Your name]'s Pumpkin Story.*

3 Place the sheets of paper between the front and back covers. Ask a grown-up to help you staple along the left side, or punch three holes along the side and bind your journal with ribbon or brass fasteners.

4 Open up your pumpkin journal to the first page, grab a pencil and some art supplies, and start dreaming, drawing, and writing!

PUMPKIN-SHAPE JOURNAL: Fold a piece of orange construction paper in half and draw a large circle on it. Cut around the circle to make the front and back covers of your book. Trace the covers onto a stack of plain white paper and cut out the pages. Then, staple the left side to bind the book together, or punch two holes in the left-hand edge of each piece of paper and bind the book together with brass fasteners, ribbon, or twine.

BE A WEATHER WATCHER!

Don't wait for the weather announcer to tell you what's going on outside: Track the weather on your own! Every day, record the outside temperature from an outdoor thermometer, and note the conditions—cloudy, sunny, or rainy. Add important details, such as a frost or thundershower. Don't forget to write down the day and date! Or, use a calendar, taped in your pumpkin journal, to record your observations.

At the end of the year, you'll have a complete weather journal!

A JOURNALING NOTE

Your pumpkin journal is *your* book of pumpkin artwork, thoughts, predictions, observations, and feelings. You decide what goes in it. There is no right or wrong way to do it. Draw whatever you like. Use creative spelling, sounding out words, to get your ideas across. The important thing is that you use the journal, and have fun!

Put on your coat and galoshes,
Cover your head with your thinking cap,
And stand where you'll garden
To plan your pumpkin patch.

Plan Your Pumpkin Plot!

Pumpkins will grow just about anywhere—in a sunny nook next to the house, in a planter on the porch, even in the compost pile. They aren't fussy. But when you're growing pumpkins for the first time, it's a good idea to start with a plan. That's especially true if you might be digging up part of the lawn for your garden! Planning is a perfect task to do in the early springtime, while you're waiting for the rain (or snow) to stop and the ground to warm and dry up enough to plant. Decide how big your plot should be and where it should go; then, draw a map of it on paper. Are you ready? Put on your boots, grab your pumpkin journal, and head outside.

SPRING

What you need:

Tape measure ◆ Sticks (each about a foot/ 30 cm long) ◆ Plenty of string ◆ Pencils, colored markers, colored pencils, or other art supplies ◆ Pumpkin journal

What you do:

1 Select a sunny spot for your garden. If your family already has a vegetable garden, all you'll need to do is claim one end of it for your pumpkin patch. If you live in an apartment, you can plant a pumpkin patch in a container out on a sunny patio or deck.

2 Once you know where your garden is going, determine its size and shape. Why not make your garden round, like a pumpkin? Pumpkin vines tend to be long and rambling, so you'll want to give them plenty of room to trail. A garden at least 3 feet by 3 feet (1 m by 1 m) will give you room for 2 or 3 plants; make it larger if you want more pumpkins. When your design is the size and shape you want, mark the edges of your garden with sticks and string.

3 Head back indoors (time for a cup of hot cocoa!). Draw a full-page picture of your pumpkin plot in your journal, matching the shape you decided on outside. If there are any landmarks, such as a big rock or a garden bench, include those in your drawing, too. And if there's something you'd like to put in your plot, like a scarecrow, add it as well.

4 Now, mark where your pumpkins will go. If you're planning on more than just pumpkins, sketch a map of your whole garden.

5 Use colored pencils or markers to color the different areas — orange for pumpkins, shades of green for beans and peas, yellow for corn, and pastels for the flowers. Wow! That's a mighty pretty garden patch!

Dream Up an "Everything Orange" Garden!

While you're planning your pumpkin patch, add some extra areas to your design to make an orange theme garden. Start with pumpkins and marigolds in the middle—the flowers will be colorful, and their strong scent may help protect your patch from roving insects. Add carrots, orange peppers, and orange flowers (such as nasturtiums) on the sides.

In the Pumpkin Journal . . .

With an orange marker or colored pencil, write and illustrate a poem about the color orange. What does orange look like? Write a list or draw pictures of everything you know that's the color orange. Basketballs, oranges, and carrots are just the beginning. How does the color orange make you feel? It might make you happy, or scared, depending on your mood. How do orange foods taste and smell? Think of some of your favorites. Now read your poem aloud. "Orange" you glad you wrote a poem about orange?

Gardening with the Three Sisters

Did you know that Native Americans planted pumpkins with corn and beans? These three crops are known as the Three Sisters. In Iroquois legend, the Three Sisters are believed to be the gift from the Sun God, who created corn, beans, and squash to keep the first people of the earth healthy. The Three Sisters were traditionally planted together in a circular mound garden, reflecting the never-ending cycle of nature. Each 3-foot-diameter (1-meter-diameter) mound included 4 to 6 corn plants in the middle,

surrounded by bean plants. Pumpkins or other winter squashes were planted along the mound's edge.

As they grow, each of the Three Sisters helps her other sisters to grow better. The pumpkin vines and leaves cover the ground like a blanket, crowding out light and thus preventing weeds from getting started. They create a prickly barrier that helps keep raccoons, deer, and other critters away from the corn. The bean plants add nutrients to the soil, helping to feed the hungry corn, while the corn makes a natural trellis for the beans to climb. It's a pretty smart setup, don't you think? Give your pumpkins some pals by growing them with corn and beans!

Pumpkin Lore

The word *squash* — which is what a pumpkin is — gets its name from the Algonquian word for squash, *askuta,* which means "sister." Some Native Americans called pumpkins *isquotersquash.* Say that five times fast!

In Native American tribes of the past, women were the pumpkin farmers. To prepare the hills for planting, they used digging sticks made of shells, sticks, rocks, antlers, or even animal bones. Planting sticks, made from a thin branch with a seed-sized tip, were used to poke the seeds into the ground.

While corn and beans are a pumpkin's pals, beware — a pumpkin's worst enemy is a potato. Plant these two crops far apart!

PUMPKIN PONDERINGS

WIDTHS AND WIGWAMS

★ In traditional Native American times, rulers and yardsticks were not used for measuring. Can you think how distances (such as a foot or yard) between plants and mounds might have been measured? Think "feet"!

★ If you grow more than one Three Sisters mound, you might want to make a space in the center of your garden for a wigwam (a tepee-shaped structure). The wigwam poles can support climbing vines, such as pole beans or morning glory flowers, or even vines for mini-pumpkins. In the hot summer, you'll have a cool, secret retreat!

Pumpkin Lore

THE SEED MAN

There once was an old man who would walk the trails picking up seeds of the Three Sisters—the squash, the bean, and the corn. He would say, "My friend, I can see that you are in need. I will take care of you."

Then, one day, the old man fell sick. He couldn't find the strength to get out of bed. Outside, he heard a woman whisper to him: "Many times you helped me and my sisters. You took care of us, so we will take care of you."

She told the man to place a cup outside. "When the rain falls, you must drink it, for the rainwater will be your medicine."

The next day, the old man put a cup made of birch bark outside. The rain filled the cup and he drank the water. When he woke up the next day, he was cured!

This story is an old tale told by the Tuscarora tribe of the Northeast. If you take care of seeds, like the old man did, the seeds will take care of you by providing you with food. Remember this story as you plant and tend your pumpkin patch!

On a day that nips your nose,
When doors and windows still are closed,
Use paper and paint for pumpkin crafts,
And bake a batch of pumpkin cookies.

Make a Paper Pumpkin Garland

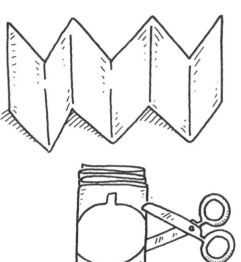

Get in the pumpkin spirit by hanging this garland in your room.

What you need:

Orange construction paper ◆ Child safety scissors ◆ Markers or paint ◆ Ruler

What you do:

1 Cut a 3-inch by 12-inch (7.5-cm by 30-cm) strip from a piece of orange construction paper. Fold up the paper, accordion-style, six times.

2 On the top layer, draw a pumpkin with a stem. Make sure the widest sides of the pumpkin go beyond the folded edge.

3 Now cut through all the layers except the sides of the pumpkin that touch the fold.

4 Open the garland, and decorate the pumpkins with markers or paint. Hang in a place for all to see.

Mix a Batch of Pumpkin Cookies

While you're waiting for the weather to warm, make these chewy cookies with canned or frozen pumpkin. When served warm with milk for dipping, they'll hit the spot on a rainy spring day, and remind you that the growing season is not far off!

What you need:

½ cup (125 ml) butter or margarine

¾ cup (175 ml) brown sugar

¼ cup (50 ml) molasses

1 egg

1 cup (250 ml) pumpkin mash (see page 72) or canned pumpkin

2 cups (500 ml) all-purpose flour

½ teaspoon (2 ml) baking soda

1 teaspoon (5 ml) baking powder

1 teaspoon (5 ml) cinnamon

½ teaspoon (2 ml) nutmeg

½ cup (125 ml) raisins or chocolate chips

What you do:

1 Preheat the oven to 350°F (180°C). In a large mixing bowl, cream the butter and sugar. Add the molasses and egg, and beat well. Beat in the pumpkin mash; set aside.

2 In a separate bowl, mix the flour, baking soda, baking powder, and spices.

3 Stir the pumpkin mixture into the flour mixture until combined. Then, mix in the raisins or chocolate chips.

4 Drop the batter by teaspoonfuls onto an ungreased cookie sheet, spacing the cookies at least 1 inch (2.5 cm) apart. Bake for 10 minutes, or until the cookies spring back when lightly pressed. Serve with a cold glass of milk.

Makes 45 mini-pumpkin cookies.

In the Pumpkin Journal . . .

Using bright markers, draw a picture in your journal of you (and anyone helping you) baking cookies. Add a window to your picture, and draw what you see outside. Date your picture.

DIGGING DEEPER... Signs of Spring

Have you spotted the first robin yet? Look for signs of spring around your house: warmer weather, birds coming back, lengthening days, buds beginning to open, bulbs shooting up, and biting insects. In your pumpkin journal, draw or make a list of spring signs you might look for. As winter turns to spring, check off what you see, smell, feel, or hear. Welcome, spring!

Think about all the different pumpkins,
The giant, the baby, the white.
How does a seed know
Which one to grow?

Pumpkins Galore!

One of the best things about pumpkins is there are so many types (called *varieties* by gardeners) to choose from. Some pumpkins, like Jack Be Little, will fit in the palm of your hand. Others, like Atlantic Giant and Big Max, may weigh more than you! There are pumpkins for every type and size of garden: big, little, even gardens in a pot. Some old-fashioned pumpkins, like Connecticut Field, need a lot of room to grow, while mini-pumpkins like Baby Boo can grow "up," on a trellis, instead!

Pumpkins aren't just orange anymore, either. Some, such as Lumina, are white on the outside. Others, like Jarrahdale, are actually gray-blue!

Turn the page for a list of pumpkins you can choose for your garden. There's an estimate of how many days each pumpkin takes to ripen and whether it's best for decorating or making pie. Look through gardening seed catalogs for more ideas of what to plant.

AUTUMN GOLD HYBRID: This pumpkin turns yellow early in the growing season. It's ready to carve or cook in about 90 days.

BABY BOO: A 95-dayer, this tiny pumpkin has a white shell that's just right for painting and decorating.

BIG MAX, PRIZEWINNER, OR DILL'S ATLANTIC GIANT: Enter these giants in a county fair. Plan on 120 days of growing time, and give them plenty of room!

CONNECTICUT FIELD: Another 120-dayer, this squash is known as the traditional American pumpkin.

GREEN-STRIPED CUSHAW: A sweet pumpkin with a green-striped neck. Give it 115 days to grow.

HOWDEN: A big, deep orange jack-o'-lantern pumpkin from Massachusetts. Another 115-dayer.

JACK BE LITTLE: Just 2 to 3 inches (5 to 7.5 cm) wide, these mini-pumpkins are fun to use for decorations. They're ready in 90 days.

JARRAHDALE: This Australian native is a spooky gray-blue on the outside but orange on the inside. Give it 100 days to get deep ribs.

LUMINA: This ghostly white pumpkin is ready to pick in 80 or 90 days.

ROUGE VIF D'ETAMPES: Cinderella rode to the ball in this French heirloom pumpkin that takes 95 to 110 days to grow.

SPOOKTACULAR: This 3- to 5-pound (1.25- to 2.25-kg) deep orange carving pumpkin is ready in 85 days.

SUGAR OR SMALL SUGAR: Thick and sweet, this is the favorite with New England pie-makers. Also called New England Pie, it's ready in 105 days.

MEET THE PUMPKIN FAMILY!

Like people, every plant has a family. The plants in a family don't necessarily look alike, but they do have some similarities, or characteristics, in common — just as you are likely to have similar habits, looks, or mannerisms with the people in *your* family. Pumpkins and other squashes, as well as plants such as cucumbers, melons, and gourds, are actually all part of the Cucurbitaceae (kew-kur-bi-TAY-see-ee) family. Can you guess some of their shared similarities? Think creeping vines, big leaves, and golden flowers — and what about the fruit? Draw or write about the family resemblances in your pumpkin journal.

You already know many of the closest pumpkin siblings by their common names: zucchini and yellow summer squash, butternut and hubbard winter squashes, acorn squash and oddities like spaghetti squash, and gourds (the warty squash used for birdhouses). A pretty interesting family, don't you think?

Pumpkin family tree

spaghetti · acorn · autumn squash · butternut · winter squash · hubbard · gourds · pumpkins · zucchini · yellow · summer squash

DIGGING DEEPER... Plot Your Family Tree!

Who is in *your* family tree? Trace the pumpkin family tree and add in your own siblings, parents, and grandparents, adding more branches as you need them. Write a caption that tells something special about your family, and tape your tree in your pumpkin journal.

When rain pours onto your plot,
And it's wet and cold outdoors,
Imagine your garden-to-be,
And buy your pumpkin seeds!

Seed Shopping Spree!

SEED SOURCES

Here's a sampling of companies that can meet your pumpkin seed needs.

* Bountiful Gardens, 18001 Shafer Ranch Rd., Willits, CA 95490-9626

* The Cook's Garden, P.O. Box 535, Londonderry, VT 05148

* Johnny's Selected Seeds, 1 Foss Hill Rd., Albion, ME 04910-9731

* Park Seed Co., 1 Parkton Ave., Greenwood, SC 29647-0001

* Shepherd's Garden Seeds, 30 Irene St., Torrington, CT 06790-6658

* Southern Exposure Seed Exchange, P.O. Box 170, Earlysville, VA 22936

* Territorial Seed Co., P.O. Box 157, Cottage Grove, OR 97424

* W. Atlee Burpee & Co., 300 Park Ave., Warminster, PA 18974

Once you decide which pumpkins you'd like to grow, you can begin shopping. Look for pumpkin seeds at your local gardening center, hardware store, even your supermarket. Or order your seeds through a seed catalog. All you need is a pen, a catalog, a stamp . . . and money for the seeds!

What you do:

1 Look through the catalogs to find the seeds you want to buy. You might want to order three different kinds: one that's especially for pie (such as Small Sugar), a mini-pumpkin variety (Jack Be Little), and a giant pumpkin (Big Max) to make into jack-o'-lanterns or to enter in a county fair.

2 Ask a grown-up to help you fill out the order form in the catalog with the item number, the price, and the quantity. Then, add the shipping and handling charges, and total your order.

3 Send for your seeds!

In the Pumpkin Journal . . .

Cut out the photos of the pumpkins you are buying seeds for and glue them into the pages of your pumpkin journal. On planting day, glue or tape a couple of seeds in your journal, and the packet that they came in. As your pumpkin vine grows through the summer, you can look back and remember the seed that started the magic!

Pumpkin Lore

Pumpkin seeds dating as far back as 7000 B.C. — that's about *9 thousand* years ago! — have been found in caves in northeastern Mexico.

PUMPKIN PONDERINGS

★ How do the prices compare in the catalogs and in the stores? Remember to add in the shipping charges as you compare.

★ Suppose you were a pumpkin farmer and you had to order seeds. For every acre, you'll need 4 pounds (8.8 kg) of pumpkin seeds. How many pounds will you need for a 10-acre patch?

The Pumpkin Seed's Story

What's inside a pumpkin seed? A good snack, or hundreds of microscopic pumpkins? To 'find out, soak the seed for several days in warm water. Watch how the seed changes as it soaks. Peel off the outer seed coat of the pumpkin seed; then, split the seed in half lengthwise with your fingernail. Can you see the tiny root, stem, leaves, and enough food for the pumpkin plant to begin its life? Draw a picture of it in your pumpkin journal. This is how your pumpkin harvest begins!

Shovel deep into the ground
(Avoiding the earthworms that help you work),
Loosen the soil
And mix in manure and magic.

Make Your Pumpkin Bed!

Y ou know how to make your own bed, but have you ever made a *pumpkin* bed? Once you've got your pumpkin patch all measured out, and the soil is dry enough to work, you're ready to get set for planting . . . and get your hands in the dirt!

What you need:

Boots ◆ A digging fork or a shovel ◆ Aged manure (available at garden supply stores) or compost ◆ Mulch ◆ Ruler or measuring tape

What you do:

1 Start with a little weeding—pull up any unwanted plants in your garden plot. If you are starting a new garden in the lawn, dig up the sod and slice off the grass. Digging is hard work, so ask a gardening grown-up to help you.

2 Next, loosen the dirt with a shovel or digging fork. Dig deep, to about a foot (30 cm), and break up all the clumps. Remove any big rocks. Your goal is to make the soil light and airy so the pumpkin roots have room to grow.

3 Now, sprinkle a few inches of aged manure or compost on top of your garden plot. Mix it in with your shovel; then, smooth out the bed. Ahhh! Those pumpkin plants are going to thank you.

WHEN SMALL IS ALL

Making your pumpkin's bed is even easier if your garden is a barrel or pot on the patio. Instead of using good old garden-variety dirt, just buy a light, fluffy soil mix for growing vegetables in pots at a garden supply store or nursery. Usually, these "growing mixes" have fertilizer (plant food) already added in, so you're ready to go!

19

When the tree leaves start to appear,
And the soil warms all the way up,
It's time to plant
Your pumpkin seeds.

Pick a Pumpkin Planting Day!

How do farmers know when to plant their pumpkin seeds? They find out when the last spring frost is expected in their area. It's called the "last frost date." A few weeks after that date, the pumpkin plants go in. By that time, all danger of frost is past. Hurrah! Pumpkins like their soil warm, at a soil temperature of about 70°F (21°C).

Visit your library or a local nursery to find out when the last spring frost is expected in your area. Or, call your local weather station. Then count the weeks, and be patient. Pumpkin planting day is almost here!

DIGGING DEEPER...

Clues from Nature

In the days before you could call up a weather station to find out the last frost date, gardeners looked for signs in nature to tell them when to plant. Some indications that the weather had warmed enough were when the white oak leaf had grown the size of a mouse's ear, or a dogwood leaf had grown the size of a squirrel's ear. What signs tell you that it's warm enough to plant pumpkins in your area? Make a note of them in your pumpkin journal, or draw a spring planting scene that includes some of these signs.

MAKE YOUR MARK!

Keep track of your pumpkin varieties with these simple garden markers. Using Popsicle sticks or tongue depressors, and orange, black, and green permanent markers, write the name of the pumpkin, such as Sugar or Big Max, on the stick. Push the marker into the soil next to the seeds on planting day.

GET A JUMP-START ON SPRING

If you live where the growing season is short, you might need to give your pumpkins a head start. About three weeks before your last spring frost, plant pumpkin seeds in peat pots (available from gardening or hardware stores) or in clean, recycled containers filled with potting soil. Cover the containers with plastic bags to keep the moisture in, and set these mini-greenhouses in a warm spot. As soon as the first seedlings appear, move the containers to a sunny window or under a light, and remove the plastic. Keep the soil moist. When there is no danger of frost in your area, gradually expose the pumpkin plants to the weather outside (called *hardening off*). Once the seedlings can safely stay out all night, they're ready to move into the garden!

Poke five little holes with your finger,
Stick in five little seeds with your thumb,
Sprinkle with water, send them a song,
And a wish to help them grow.

Ready, Set, Plant!

Grab a hoe and your seeds, and head to the garden. It's pumpkin planting time!

What you need:

Pumpkin seeds or seedlings ◆ Hoe ◆
Tape measure or ruler ◆ Water

What you do:

1 Using your plan in the pumpkin journal as a guide, form the prepared garden soil into small circular planting areas, called *hills*. The spacing will depend on the type of pumpkins you grow. For old-fashioned pumpkins, allow about 6 feet (2 m) between circles; most other pumpkins can go closer together, say, 3 feet (1 m) apart. To plant a garden in a container, sow the seeds as if you were making one hill.

2 Poke 5 holes in each hill with your fingers, each about an inch (2.5 cm) deep. Place a seed in each hole and cover with soil.

3 Sprinkle with water like a gentle rain.

WAKE UP, SEEDS! With the extra seeds left over from planting your pumpkins, plant a few pumpkins in containers of potting soil. Water them well, and put them in a warm spot. As you wait for your garden seeds to sprout, dig up the potted pumpkin seeds, to see what is going on underground!

Give a Planting Day Party!

You can carry on Native American planting customs by making Pumpkin Patch Muffins (see page 24) and inviting family and friends over for a special planting day ceremony. As you put each seedling or seed in the ground, wish it well and thank the earth for helping it to grow. Can you think of other ways to celebrate planting day? Sing this song to get you started!

THE PUMPKIN SEED SONG
(to the tune of *London Bridge*)

See my little pumpkin seed, pumpkin seed, pumpkin seed
See my little pumpkin seed
Now I'll plant it.
Water it and watch it grow, watch it grow, watch it grow
Water it and watch it grow
In my garden.
When it grows up big like me, big like me, big like me
When it grows up big like me
Then I'll pick it.

Pumpkin Lore

APACHE PUMPKIN CEREMONY

When the very first pumpkin vines sprouted in the fields, the Apache Indians sent a small boy out to collect juniper berries in the forest. Upon his return, they blindfolded the boy and guided him to the pumpkin patch. There, he was told to toss the berries up toward the sky. Wherever the berries landed, the Apaches hoped a giant pumpkin would grow!

Pumpkin Patch Muffins

These moist, wholesome muffins will give you energy for planting day.

What you need:

- 1 cup (250 ml) pumpkin mash (see page 72) or canned pumpkin
- ½ cup (125 ml) packed brown sugar
- ¼ cup (50 ml) melted butter or margarine
- 2 eggs
- ¾ cup (175 ml) milk
- 2 cups (500 ml) all-purpose flour (or 1 cup/ 250 ml all-purpose and 1 cup/250 ml wheat flour)
- 2 teaspoons (10 ml) baking powder
- ½ teaspoon (2 ml) salt

What you do:

1. Preheat the oven to 375°F (190°C). In a large mixing bowl or bowl of an electric mixer, mix or blend the pumpkin mash, brown sugar, melted butter, and eggs. Then, add the milk.

2. In a separate mixing bowl, sift the flour with the baking powder and salt.

3. Add the dry ingredients to the pumpkin mixture and stir or blend until just combined.

4. Spoon the batter into a 12-cup muffin tin lined with paper liners. Bake the muffins for 20 minutes. Serve with jam or butter.

Makes 10 to 12 breakfast treats for planting day.

PUMPKIN-CHOCOLATE CHIP MUFFINS: Stir ½ cup (125 ml) chocolate chips into the batter.

PUMPKIN-RAISIN MUFFINS: Stir ½ cup (125 ml) raisins into the batter.

PUMPKIN SPICE MUFFINS: Sift ½ teaspoon (2 ml) cinnamon and ¼ teaspoon (1 ml) nutmeg with the flour in step 2.

Pumpkin Lore

In colonial times, pumpkins were such a favorite food that the Port of Boston was called Pumpkinshire!

Pumpkin Crayon Suncatcher

Make this bright suncatcher to welcome the longer daylight of summer.

What you need:

Orange and green crayons ◆ Pencil sharpener or cheese grater ◆ Waxed paper ◆ Iron ◆ Scissors ◆ String and tape

What you do:

1 Sharpen the orange and green crayons and collect the shavings. Or, you can ask a grown-up to help you grate the crayons on a cheese grater.

2 Sprinkle the orange shavings on a sheet of waxed paper, so that they resemble a round pumpkin.

Sprinkle the green shavings at the top for the pumpkin stem. Cover with a second sheet of waxed paper.

3 Ask a grown-up to help you iron the waxed paper "sandwich" on a low setting until the shavings melt, about 5 to 8 seconds.

4 Use the scissors to trim around the pumpkin. Then, tape a loop of string to the pumpkin stem. Hang your suncatcher in a sunny window to capture the sun's rays.

The Pumpkin Seed's Story

The pumpkin seed you planted lies quietly in the warm soil. The rain and water from the sprinkling can bathes it gently. The seed soaks in the water, slowly waking up. Get up, seed! It's time to start growing!

SUMMER

Pumpkin Care, Crafts, and "Cool" Cooking

In summer, you watch the magic of the garden unfold as the seeds you've planted grow first into seedlings; then, into pumpkin vines with pumpkins that get big, bigger, and biggest in the sun. The garden projects you'll find here will help you become the caretaker of your pumpkin patch and explore the life of the plants from sprout to giant pumpkin. Add to the adventure by making your own homemade garden garb! And you'll find plenty of cool summer treats to keep you going as you tend your plants. You can water, weed, mulch, and feed them . . . maybe even sing them a song! Along the way, you'll be helped by bees, rain, sun, and the "good bugs" in the soil. All the players in your garden's web of life—especially you—have an important part to perform. Get ready, the show is about to begin!

Watch each day get a little longer
And sun flood your garden with light,
As the seeds sprout
And the first leaves appear.

Create a Seed-Sprout Flip-Book!

Remember that pumpkin seed you glued or taped inside your pumpkin journal? You can make it sprout and grow, mimicking the pumpkin seeds in the garden, by making a seed-sprout flip-book. You'll need a 4-inch by 6-inch (10-cm by 15-cm) notepad of unlined paper with at least 20 sheets in it.
On the last page, draw a pumpkin seed in the corner, at the bottom of the page. On the next-to-last page, in the same corner, draw the seed with a small root emerging, just as you noticed the seeds growing. Continue drawing as you watch your plant grow, adding the vine as it appears, the first flower and tiny pumpkin, and finally a big pumpkin. Fill all 20 pages. Now flip the pages, and watch the moving picture of your growing pumpkin!

PUMPKIN JOURNAL FLIP-BOOK: Make a pumpkin seed flip-book in the lower right-hand corner of your journal. Start with the last page of your journal, and move back toward the front with your picture story.

The Pumpkin Seed's Story

As the pumpkin seed swells with moisture, it grows its roots, reaching deep for water and the food in the soil. Finally, the green baby leaves *(cotyledons)* sprout above the soil. Yeah, seed! You did it! Welcome to the world! Look closely: As the baby leaves grow, they might wear the seed as a cap. Silly pumpkin seed! Pretty soon the pumpkin sprout has "true" leaves above the baby leaves. These lobed leaves with veins are reaching for the sky, toward sun and rain. Now you're really starting to grow, pumpkin sprout!

DIGGING DEEPER...   Pumpkin Seeds Up Close

Want to see what's going on underground? After one week of waiting, dig up that first extra seed that you planted in peat pots back when you put your seeds in the ground outdoors. Maybe you see just roots, or perhaps the start of the leaves. Sketch it in your journal, and include the date. After another week, dig up the second extra peat pot and examine the seed. Has it sprouted yet? Outdoors in your pumpkin garden, find the pumpkin's first true leaves. What shape and colors do you see? Look closely around the pumpkin's stem and leaf to find the pumpkin plant's prickly protection. Ouch! Don't squeeze too tight!

Scarecrows Alive!

*C*hase away hungry birds with this clever scarecrow. If you're making it in early summer, follow the Milk Jug-Head Scarecrow directions. Once you've harvested your first pumpkin, you can substitute a real pumpkin for the milk jug. Or, use a pillowcase head stuffed with straw.

What you need:

1 large pumpkin ◆ Hammer and nails ◆ Pushpins ◆ Sticks, corncobs, and other natural items for the pumpkin's features ◆ Glue or glue gun ◆ 1 3-foot (1 m) stick or branch ◆ 1 6-foot (2 m) wooden stake with pointed ends ◆ Old clothes ◆ Straw or wads of old newspaper

What you do:

1 Decorate the pumpkin to look like a scarecrow's head. Using a hammer and nail or a screwdriver, poke holes in the top of the pumpkin. Insert small sticks in the holes for a head of spiked hair. Use pushpins to add squash or gourds, cut in half, for eyes. Glue on a corncob for the nose. A bent stick makes a perfect crooked smile.

2. Make a cross for the scarecrow's body by hammering the 3-foot-long (1 m) stick perpendicular to the 6-foot-long (2 m) stake. Ask a grown-up to help you. Dress the wooden figure in old clothes, and stuff it with wadded newspaper or straw. Push the stake about 1 foot (30 cm) into the ground.

3. Push the pumpkin head on top of the stake until the point almost reaches the top of the pumpkin. This can be tricky: Ask a grown-up to help. Now watch the birds fly away as Pumpkin Head does his work!

MILK JUG-HEAD SCARECROW: Turn a clean, gallon-size (4-liter) milk jug upside down so the bottom of the jug makes the forehead of the scarecrow. Paint on eyes, nose, and a grin (or a scary grimace) with orange acrylic paint. Once the paint has dried, follow the directions for steps 2 and 3 above, but use the milk jug pumpkin instead of a real pumpkin.

STRAW-HEAD SCARECROW: Use an old, plain-colored pillowcase for the head. Stuff it with straw or wadded newspaper. Tape up the extra material on the pillowcase until you have a head shape you like. Paint a face on the front of the head, and let it dry for an hour or so. Attach the straw head to the stake and tuck the bottom of the tied pillowcase into the scarecrow's shirt. Place a hat on top of your scarecrow's head, and you're done.

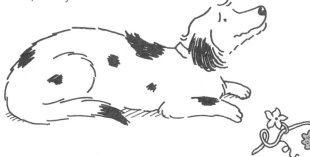

Pumpkin Lore

Scarecrows have been around for some 2,500 years! Ancient Greeks carved scarecrows out of wood and gave them ugly, twisted-looking faces. European farmers made witchlike scarecrows, and Japanese scarecrows from long ago held a bow and arrow.

In the Pumpkin Journal . . .

* Take a photograph of your scarecrow. Glue it into the pages of your journal. Write down your scarecrow's birthdate. Then, watch your creation in action. Does your scarecrow scare anything away?

* Using brightly colored crayons, completely cover a page of your journal. Next, cover the whole page with black crayon. Use a toothpick to scratch out a picture about a scarecrow who comes to life in the middle of the night. Write a caption to your picture, and date it.

Thin Those Sprouts!

Once the pumpkin sprouts are about 4 inches (10 cm) tall and have 4 or 5 true leaves, they're ready to make it on their own. Dig up the weakest plants, leaving two pumpkin plants per hill. Or snip off the tops of the rejects with a pair of scissors. Good gardeners do this process, called *thinning*, with all their crops. If you leave all the plants in one spot, they'll be too crowded, and you won't get pumpkins!

Before you go outside to water, weed, and tend,
Dress in your pumpkin shirt and hat,
Or some old clothes that look,
Like a scarecrow's.

Sponge-Print a Pumpkin T-Shirt

What you need:

Cardboard ◆ White T-shirt ◆ Masking tape
Sponge ◆ Orange fabric paint ◆ Paper plate
Green puffy fabric paint ◆ Paintbrush
Fabric markers ◆ Iron

What you do:

1 Place a piece of cardboard into the body of the T-shirt. Fold the sleeves back and tape the shirt with masking tape so you have a flat surface.

2 Ask a grown-up to help you cut the sponge into a pumpkin-shaped stamp. Or, cut different sizes.

3 Pour the orange fabric paint onto the paper plate. (If the paint is thick, thin it down with a few drops of water.) Dip the sponge into the paint; then, stamp it onto the T-shirt. Stamp as many pumpkins as you want.

4 Add vines with the green puffy fabric paint.

5 Write your name with a paintbrush or fabric marker, and write anything else you want to write, like "My Pumpkin Patch."

6 Let the T-shirts dry flat for 24 hours. Then, turn them inside-out and ask a grown-up to help you iron them to heat-set the paint.

SUNNY PUMPKIN SNEAKS: Decorate a pair of white sneakers with orange and green fabric paint. You can buy an inexpensive pair at a discount store or use an old pair of white canvas sneaks that you've run through the wash. Now, walk through your pumpkin patch in style!

Put On a Pumpkin Hat!

Every gardener needs a hat for protection from the hot sun.

What you need:

White baseball cap ◆ Orange fabric paint (available from art supply stores) ◆ Green fabric paint ◆ Paintbrush ◆ Green pipecleaner ◆ Green felt

What you do:

1. Use the fabric paint to thoroughly paint the baseball hat orange (except for the bill — leave it white). Paint grooves with a darker orange paint. Then, write your name on the bill of the hat with the green paint, paint on a few smaller pumpkins, and add a vine to connect them.

2. Once the paint dries (after about 24 hours), add a pipecleaner vine to the top of the hat. Cut small leaves out of the felt. Cut a tiny hole on one end of each leaf; then, thread them onto the pipecleaner vine. Twist the pipecleaner to look like a real vine.

3. Attach the vine to the top of the baseball hat by wrapping one end around the button at the top of the hat. Or, poke a hole through the top of the hat, slip the pipecleaner vine through the hole, and cover the end with masking tape.

QUICK PAPER HAT: In a hurry for a hat? Grab yesterday's newspaper. Unfold 5 sheets of newspaper and stack them together. Now put them over your head, and have a friend wrap masking tape around the crown of your hat, on your forehead. Remove the hat and trim the corners. Make the brim any size you like! Then, staple the newspaper edges together, or roll up the brim and staple it in place. Decorate your hat with whatever you like. If you used the Sunday Comics, you're all set — but don't be surprised if other gardeners stop to get a laugh!

In the Pumpkin Journal . . .

Have someone take a photo of you wearing your pumpkin hat, T-shirt, and sneaks, and glue it in your journal. Mark the date, and write a caption. Pretty cool duds!

Pumpkins don't ask for much from the gardener. Sun, good soil, and water keep them content. Watch the pumpkins grow, and give them a helping hand if they need it. Be like the ancient Chinese Taoist god Shou-xing, in the story below, and your plants will thank you with a hefty harvest!

Pumpkin Lore

THE STORY OF SHOU-XING

When Shou-xing was a boy, he was told that he would have only 19 more years to live. Around the time of his 19th birthday, he was advised to go to an open field and bring with him food and drink. When he arrived, he found two men under a mulberry tree. He offered them the food and drink.

The men were very grateful to Shou-xing. To show their appreciation for his hospitality, they offered to reverse the digits of the boy's age. Instead of 19, Shou-xing lived until he was 91!

The legendary Shou-xing, who became the ancient Chinese Taoist god of Long Life and Luck, is often pictured carrying a long staff and a pumpkin, filled with the water of life.

Water the thirsty new plants,
And pull weeds with all your might.
A layer of mulch will ease your task,
So you can sing, dance, and play the summer away.

Watering Wisdom

Pumpkins, like us, need lots and lots of water to grow. In fact, 90 percent (almost all) of a pumpkin is water! To keep these big drinkers happy, follow these tips:

❋ Give young plants a daily soak if needed to help get them started. Stick your finger in the soil to see if it has dried out beneath the surface. If it has, water it! Follow your garden hunches: If a plant is wilting, it's probably thirsty!

❋ The best time of day to water pumpkins (and other garden plants) is in the early morning. That's when plants do a lot of their growing! The heat isn't as strong at that time of day, so the water will stay in the soil when you add it.

❋ Be a gentle rain shower, watering gently with a watering can or sprinkler.

Mulching Madness

Mulch is like a comfy blanket for your garden. It keeps the weeds from growing and the soil moist and soft, perfect for making pumpkin roots happy and for coaxing along young plants. Use a 2-inch (5 cm) layer of leaves, dried grass clippings, straw (seed-free hay), or bark mulch to tuck in around your garden. Or, lay sheets of black-and-white newspaper in your garden, and cover them with mulch. You won't need to weed all summer!

Weeding Out Weeds

Weeds are the uninvited guests of your pumpkin plants. Like too many people at a party, weeds can crowd your plants. What do you do? Pull 'em out! The best time to weed is after a soaking rain, when the plants are dry but the ground is still damp and the roots are easy to pull. Be sure you know which plants are weeds and which are your pumpkins!

Celebrate Summer!

Taking care of a garden is a great way to enjoy the sunshine. When you garden, bring along plenty of sunscreen, a hat to shade your head, and a jug of lemonade to quench your thirst. On a hot summer day, garden with your feet bare, wiggling your toes in the soil. Whistle a gardening song! Do a dance in the garden! Turn on the sprinkler and dash through the grass in your swimsuit. Then, find a special spot in your garden for a cool retreat, and sit back to watch the garden grow!

39

Pumpkin Ice Cream Pie

Though pumpkin pie is usually thought of as a fall celebration food, it makes for good eating any time of year. Try this no-cook pie for a cool summer treat.

What you need:

CRUST

1½ cups (375 ml) crushed gingersnap cookies or graham crackers

6 tablespoons (75 ml) butter or margarine, melted

FILLING

1 quart (1 liter) vanilla ice cream or frozen yogurt

1 cup (250 ml) pumpkin mash (see page 72) or canned pumpkin

¼ cup (50 ml) sugar

1 teaspoon (5 ml) cinnamon

¼ teaspoon (1 ml) ginger

What you do:

1 To make the crust, mix the crushed gingersnaps with the melted butter. Press it into the bottom and sides of a 9-inch (22.5-cm) pie plate.

2 Scoop the ice cream or frozen yogurt into a large mixing bowl and let it get almost soupy. Add the pumpkin mash, sugar, cinnamon, and ginger. Stir well.

3 Spoon the ice cream into the prepared gingersnap crust. Cover with plastic wrap.

4 Set the pie in a level part of your freezer and let it harden for several hours.

Serves 8 to 10 pumpkin friends.

PUMPKIN ICE CREAM SANDWICHES: Pour the pumpkin ice cream filling into a 13- by 9- by 2-inch (32.5- by 22.5- by 5-cm) baking pan and freeze. Using a sharp knife (ask a grown-up to help), cut the ice cream into graham-cracker-size pieces. Sandwich them between two graham crackers, wrap in plastic, and freeze until ready to eat!

Watch for huge flowers to blossom,
Flowers as big as your hand
That open in the bright morning sun.
Look closely at the vine and watch the magic unfold.

The Pumpkin Seed's Story

The pumpkin seed has gone from seed to sprout to vine. Now what's blooming on the pumpkin vine? Hello, pumpkin flowers! Can you tell them apart? The mother flower has a small, round green ball behind the blossom and a sticky star-like spot, or *stigma*, inside the flower. There is a long *stamen* covered with golden pollen inside the father flower. Who is hovering around the pumpkin flowers? It's a bee, coming to harvest the pollen. As the bee forages in the flowers, some of the pollen it already collected falls onto the sticky stigma of the mother flower. That's a tricky way to get around, pumpkin pollen!

PUMPKIN PONDERINGS

YUMMY LEAVES!

A pumpkin plant gets nutrients and water from the soil through its roots. Meanwhile, the plant's leaves use sunlight, water, and air to make food for the plant. It's sort of like a mini-factory. The whole process is called *photosynthesis.* Expert pumpkin growers estimate that each leaf on a pumpkin vine can feed up to 4 pounds (1.74 kg) of pumpkin fruit. That's a lot of work for one leaf!

In the Pumpkin Journal . . .

Visit your garden early in the morning, when the insects are most active, and quietly watch what happens. Look closely at the golden flowers as they bloom (use a magnifying glass to get an even better look). Aren't they bright and colorful? Smell the pollen on the flower. But don't get too close, or you'll have pollen on your nose! Take a photograph of a bee bringing pollen to a pumpkin flower. Paste it into the pages of your journal, with the date and a caption. Or draw a cartoon of the visiting bee. What might it be thinking as it dips and dives for pollen?

Pumpkin Lore

FLOWER FUN

The Pueblo Indians of the Southwest often work pumpkin blossom designs into silver jewelry. The blossoms are an important source of food, too. When Pueblo and Hopi farmers harvest their pumpkins at the end of the growing season, they also gather all the leftover flowers that will never turn into squash, and fry them with cornmeal and egg. Yum!

When fireflies fly in the night
Some blossoms turn into pumpkins,
Small, tiny pumpkins
That grow big, bigger, and biggest.

The Pumpkin Seed's Story

You've come a long way, pumpkin seed! The roots of your vine are reaching into the earth for water and nutrients, and your leaves are busy making food for the plant from sunshine and water. The prickly pumpkin vine bends over and travels, and a curling tendril reaches out. Now that the mother flower has its pollen, the little green globe beneath it begins to grow. Grow, pumpkins, grow!

Grow a Giant Pumpkin!

Want to grow a pumpkin that is really big? You can help your plants along with these tips from the pumpkin experts.

1 To get a big pumpkin, you need the right seeds. Plant a large pumpkin variety, such as Big Max, Prizewinner, or Atlantic Giant. Get your pumpkin growing early by starting the seeds in peat pots about 3 weeks before the last predicted spring frost. Plant them out to the garden as soon as they have their first true leaves.

2 Once the flowers appear, look for the first mother flowers. As the tiny pumpkins appear, choose the best one on each vine. Trim off all the other pumpkins on that vine.

3 When these pumpkins reach the size of basketballs, remove all but one from each plant. Choose the one that is growing the fastest, is tall, and has a round shape. Then, use scissors or pruning shears to cut back the vine so it grows only about 10 feet (3 m) beyond your chosen pumpkin.

4 Feed your plants once a week with plant food or fertilizer, and water them if it's dry. Then watch your giant pumpkins grow and grow!

FINE VINE

Guide the pumpkin vine to where you want it to wander. Every couple of feet, cover a bit of the growing vine with soil, so that more roots can grow.

PLEASE DO <u>FEED</u> THE PUMPKINS!

Pumpkins will do fine on their own in good garden soil, but like us, they enjoy an extra snack or two. You can give them a high-energy meal by watering each vine with a gallon of diluted liquid fertilizer (such as fish emulsion). Or you can "sidedress" your plants. Just lay a shovelful of rich compost or aged manure, or a sprinkling of fertilizer, around the base of each plant once the flowers have blossomed and the tiny pumpkins begin to grow. Your pumpkins will appreciate the snack!

The Great Pumpkin Contest!

☆ Want to enter your pumpkin in a contest? Call your local county cooperative extension service and find a county fair near you that has a contest. Or, enter your pumpkin in the World Pumpkin Confederation Weigh-Offs, held every year in sites throughout the world. Gardeners — including kids — enter their 100-, 400-, and even 1,000-pound (45-, 180-, 450-kg) pumpkins! For more information, contact the World Pumpkin Confederation, 14050 Rt. 62, Collins, New York 14034; phone 1-800-449-5681.

☆ In *Farmer Boy* by Laura Ingalls Wilder, Almanzo grows a prizewinning pumpkin — by feeding it milk!

Pumpkin Lore

Giant pumpkins (the ones that weigh 400 pounds/180 kg or more when they're harvested) can grow as much as 25 pounds/ 11 kg in one day! That means in two or three days they may weigh as much as you do!

The world's largest pumpkin was grown by Nathan and Paula Zehr from Watson, New York, in 1996. It weighed 1,061 pounds (477 kg) — about what a small car weighs! A 4-pound (1.75-kg) pumpkin makes enough pumpkin mash for two pies. Think of how many pies you could bake with a 1,000-pound (450-kg) pumpkin!

Silly Oddball Pumpkins

Have you ever seen a pear-shaped pumpkin? What about a square one? With a few plastic containers or an old rope, you can make a few oddballs in your pumpkin patch.

What you do:

1 When the pumpkin is round and green, tie a rope or cord around its middle. The pumpkin will grow around the cord, and when it's ripe, it will have a curvy waistline.

2 For a rectangular pumpkin, slip the growing green pumpkin into a half-gallon (2-liter) milk carton. As the pumpkin grows, it will fill up the carton. When it's ripe and orange, carefully cut the carton off the rectangular pumpkin.

3 Fashion other shapes out of cardboard boxes and masking tape. Grow oddball pumpkins to suit your imagination!

Pumpkin Tattoos!

Grow your own personalized pumpkin, with your name tattooed on the side! Or personalize one for a friend, a grandparent, or someone special. Choose a pumpkin that is still young and has buttery soft skin. Gently scratch the surface of the pumpkin with a pen, writing initials or words or a drawing or shape. As the pumpkins grow, so will your tattoos! In the fall, give your personalized present to a friend.

Watch the vines spread across your garden,
But don't let them wander too far,
Watch, pamper, and protect them
As the green pumpkins grow ripe.

The Pumpkin Seed's Story

Under the summer sun, the prickly pumpkin vine forms a carpet of leaves. Beneath the carpet, the ground is moist, shaded from the hot summer sun. Earthworms like this shady spot in the cool soil. A toad takes a rest under the shady leaves as it searches for bugs to munch for lunch. On the vine, the green pumpkins are big, and getting riper every day. Look how much you've grown, pumpkin seed! The skin of the pumpkin is getting harder. Soon it will begin to change color, to all shades of green and yellow and orange. Silly mottled pumpkin! Inside, unseen, new seeds wait, cradled in stringy hammocks.

Track Your Vine!

Pumpkin vines grow long and strong to support the growing pumpkin. The vine can grow across your yard, up a fence, or even over a wheelbarrow left too long in the garden! In small gardens, the tendrils that curl and coil from the stalk can be trained to grab onto a trellis.

What you need:

Graph paper ◆ Pencil ◆ Tape measure

What you do:

1　Along the left-hand side of a piece of graph paper, chart the numbers 1 foot (.5 m) through 20 feet (6.5 m). Along the bottom of the piece of graph paper, fill in the date.

2　On the same day of each week (say, every Tuesday), carefully measure the length of the main pumpkin vine with the tape measure. Measure the length of the runners. Add those numbers together to get the total length of vine. Then, plot the total vine measurement on the graph paper, above the correct date. Connect the dots with a line.

3　At the end of the summer, when you're done with your graph, look it over. When were the vines the longest? At what point in the summer did the vines grow the fastest? And finally, was your patch big enough to hold the sprawling vines?

PUMPKIN PONDERINGS

ROUND AND ROUND THE PUMPKIN

Keep track of how big your pumpkins are growing by measuring around them at their widest point every week, using a cloth tape measure (look in a sewing basket for one). Plot the width in your pumpkin journal. What might cause the pumpkins to grow more quickly one week or slow down one week?

In the Pumpkin Journal . . .

What might happen if the garden and the pumpkin vine were magic, as in "Jack and the Beanstalk"? Write or dictate your story (call it "[Your Name] and the Magic Pumpkin Vine"). What might happen to you in the story? Use colored pencils to illustrate your tale, and put the date on your drawing.

DIGGING DEEPER . . . Who's in the Pumpkin Patch?

The ladybugs, toads, lizards, earthworms, wasps, bees, and snakes in your garden are friendly. In fact, they help your garden stay healthy by eating "bad" bugs and pollinating the pumpkin flowers. Ask a grown-up to help you find a book on identifying garden insects and wildlife. There are only a couple of visitors, such as the wormy white squash vine borer and the disease-spreading squash bug, that can't be trusted. Look for them hiding beneath the pumpkin's prickly leaves.

Take a Pumpkin Adventure!

Here's a good activity for a warm summer evening. Invite a friend or family member over for an outdoor camp-out like Linus had in the Charlie Brown video *It's the Great Pumpkin!* Set up your tent near the pumpkin patch and snuggle up in your sleeping bag or bedroll. Don't forget to bring along a flashlight! The next day, write about, or draw, your adventure in your pumpkin journal. How did it feel to sleep out? What was the best part?

Watercolor a Pumpkin

Paint a picture of the pumpkins in your patch every few days, as they change color from deep green to harvest orange. They may ripen faster than you think!

What you need:

Large piece of cardboard ◆ Giant paper clip
White paper ◆ Paintbrush ◆ Watercolors

What you do:

1 Ask a grown-up to help you cut the cardboard into an easel. Attach the paper clip at the top and clip on a piece of paper.

2 Find a good place to sit near the garden and start painting.

3 Each pumpkin may have a different shade of green to orange. Mix a few watercolors together to match the pumpkin colors.

4 When your painting dries, put a date on it and hang it in a place for all to see.

Very Cool Pumpkins

Cool off and practice your pumpkin-carving skills with this frozen treat.

What you need:

4 to 6 oranges
1 pint (500 ml) orange sherbet
Cinnamon sticks

What you do:

1 With the help of a grown-up, cut the tops from the oranges and set them aside. Using a knife to loosen the edges, ask a grown-up to help you scoop out the inside of the orange with a spoon (save the insides to make fresh orange juice). Cut out two eyes and a nose to make the orange look like a jack-o'-lantern.

2 Spoon the sherbet into the carved oranges.

3 Cut a hole in the top of each orange and add a piece of cinnamon stick for a stem. Place the tops over the sherbet "pumpkins." Freeze until ready to eat.

Makes 4 to 6 chilly mini-pumpkin treats.

PUMPKIN SMILES: While you have some oranges on hand, ask a grown-up to help you cut one into quarters. Eat the orange from the rind, then cut it into teeth. Slip it under your lips and give a pumpkin smile!

FRUIT SALAD PUMPKINS: Mix the insides of the oranges with chopped fruit, such as melons, strawberries, apples, and bananas. Fill the carved oranges with the fruit salad instead of the sherbet.

Pumpkin Lore

The word *pumpkin* comes from the French word *pompion*, which means "ripened by the sun." It also comes from the Latin word *pepo*, meaning "a kind of melon."

FALL

Pumpkin Harvest, Celebrations, Lore . . . and Pie!

You've watered and weeded your pumpkins and watched them grow big. Now, at the end of the summer, all that tender care pays off. Under the withering, prickly pumpkin vines, your bright orange (or shining white) pumpkins are practically yelling to be picked! This is a time for celebration, and a time for thanking the soil and sun and rain for helping you along. Jump for joy! Throw a pumpkin harvest party in your neighborhood, carve and decorate your pumpkins, and cook up some healthy pumpkin recipes (you can even toast the seeds!). The activities that follow will lead you through the celebration and help you give thanks for the harvest season. Plus, you'll explore the history of some of our common pumpkin traditions: Why do we light jack-o'-lanterns, for instance, and who was "Jack" anyway? The pumpkin patch, bursting with its harvest bounty, is waiting for you. Let the fun and frolicking begin!

Look under the browning pumpkin carpet
For brilliant orange (or white) pumpkins,
Pampered by your summer care
Now ready to pick.

Pumpkin Harvest!

Your pumpkins will be ready to pick 80 to 120 days after sowing, depending on which variety you planted. How many days has it been? Look back in your pumpkin journal to your planting day! That seed that you put in the ground so long ago has been transformed into a plant, a vine, a pumpkin . . . and now it's ready to be harvested. Withered vines are a sign that your plant is getting tired and is beginning to die back.

What you need:

Small knife or garden scissors ◆ Ruler

What you do:

1. Examine the pumpkin. Is it orange (or white) on all sides? If it is, good. Now thump the shell: A pumpkin that's ready to be picked will sound hollow (empty) inside and feel hard on the outside. A dull, heavy sound signals that the pumpkin needs a little more time on the vine. If a freezing frost threatens before your pumpkins are ready, tuck the fruits in with a blanket or tarp at night.

2. Once the pumpkin is ready, cut it off the vine, using a knife or scissors. Leave about 3 inches (7.5 cm) of the stem on the pumpkin. The stem may seem like an ideal handle for carrying your pumpkin, but don't be fooled into holding it that way:

The stem of a ripe pumpkin falls off easily, and without it, your pumpkin might get moldy.

3. Brush away the dirt; then, hose off your prize pumpkin with water. Now show it to a friend. Congratulations! You did it, you really grew a pumpkin (or two)!

The Pumpkin Seed's Story

Now the pumpkin is ripe. The stem stands proud above the pumpkin. Way to go, pumpkin seed! You made it all the way on your journey to pumpkinhood!

In the Pumpkin Journal . . .

* Have someone take your picture, with you holding (or next to) your pumpkin, and frame it in your pumpkin journal, with a caption and the date. Hey, that's an impressive harvest!

* Write a five-line poem about your pumpkin, using one of your senses —sight, smell, touch, hearing, taste—for each line.

Plan a neighborhood pumpkin fair
When leaves are turning golden.
Invite friends and family
For fall fun.

Throw a Pumpkin Carnival!

On a crisp, autumn day, head outside for this fun fall festival. First, gather as many pumpkins as you can find—some small and some big. If you didn't grow enough in your garden, you can find them at farm stands, garden centers, or grocery stores. Paint signs for each of the events and invite friends and neighbors to join you in a pumpkin harvest hoe-down!

FOOD

HOST A HARVEST TASTING ◆ As part of your harvest celebration, ask each person attending your harvest party to bring food made from a harvest crop. You eat these foods all the time! Fresh apples could be one idea, or something made from apples. Applesauce, dried apple chips, or cider will do just fine. Can you think of other harvest foods made from corn, tomatoes, melons, grapes, or squash? If you're imagining foods like pumpkin pie, cornbread, pizza, pickles, popcorn, and watermelon, you're on the right track.

FALL

TEAM ACTIVITIES

PUMPKIN SLALOM RACE ◆ Divide the party into two teams. Scatter two rows of pumpkins from a starting line (each row should be about 15 yards/15 meters long). The first player weaves through the row of pumpkins, returns to the finish line, and tags the next person in line. The first team to have all its players run through the pumpkin slalom wins.

NO-HANDS PUMPKIN PIE-EATING CONTEST ◆ Every player gets a piece of the pie in this tasty harvest game. Bake one Mini-Pumpkin Pie (see page 76) per contestant. Set the pies outside on a picnic or long table. A judge should instruct each player to sit on his hands. When the players hear "Go," they race to eat their pies. The first clean pie plate wins.

PUMPKIN ROLLING RACE ◆ In this Early American game, colonial kids would push pumpkins with large wooden spoons. But you can use a broom or a stick or even just your hands to do the trick. About 15 yards (15 m) away from the starting line, place a hay bale or other large marker. Give each player a pumpkin (the small pie pumpkins work best) and a broom or stick. When the judge says "Go," players push their pumpkins around the marker and back to the starting line. No carrying allowed!

PUMPKIN RING TOSS ◆ Can you ring a hula hoop around a pumpkin? Mark a scoring point on three to five pumpkins, with the highest score farthest from the starting line. Players should stand at the line and toss the hula hoop around the pumpkins. Three tries will be plenty, and the highest scorer wins.

AUTUMN SCAVENGER HUNT ◆ This autumn, don't miss the show as nature gets ready for winter. Divide into two teams and head outside to hunt for the following items: 2 squirrels, 6 cornstalks, 5 red leaves, 6 decorated pumpkins or jack-o'-lanterns, 1 ticket stub for a county fair, 1 acorn, 5 bales of hay, and 2 different seeds. Work together with your team to spot the most items on the list. After 30 minutes, the team who has spotted the most items wins.

PUMPKIN HARVEST MURAL ◆ Cover a picnic table with newspaper and white mural paper (tape down the paper with masking tape so it doesn't blow away). Set out markers, tempera paints, and paintbrushes. Draw scenes that show what happens around harvest time in your community. Note what else is going on, too, such as apple picking or berry harvesting. What are animals, such as squirrels and chipmunks, gathering? Put your harvest mural up for others to see when it is done.

FALL

THREE SISTERS SIX-LEGGED RACE ◆

Divide the group into two teams, and each team into groups of three players, representing the corn, beans, and pumpkins from the Three Sisters garden. Tie each group of three together by their legs, using bandannas. Place a pumpkin at the end of the course. At the word "Go," have one group from each team run to the pumpkin and back. The first team to have all its players complete the course wins.

GUESSING GAMES

◆ How many seeds in a pumpkin? Take a guess. Write your guess and your name on a slip of paper and put it in a box. At the end of the carnival, cut open the pumpkin and have everyone help you divide the seeds into piles of 5 or 10 and count the piles. Whose guess was the closest? Give the winner the seeds to take home and toast!

◆ How much does a pumpkin weigh? Set aside your largest pumpkin. Have contestants lift the pumpkin and write down their guesses on a slip of paper, along with their name. At the end of the carnival, weigh the pumpkin on a scale. Give the giant pumpkin to the person whose guess was closest to the real thing.

◆ Guess the circumference! Challenge math wizards to guess the circumference (the distance around the fattest part of a pumpkin) and write it down on a slip of paper. At the end of the carnival, use a tape measure to find the actual distance. Award the pumpkin to the closest guesser.

Pumpkin Cornbread

Nothing beats a warm slice of this wholesome bread on a chilly fall day.

What you need:

1 cup (250 ml) flour

1 cup (250 ml) cornmeal

2 teaspoons (10 ml) baking powder

½ teaspoon (2 ml) salt

1 egg

¾ cup (175 ml) milk

⅓ cup (75 ml) honey

2 tablespoons (25 ml) butter, melted

½ cup (125 ml) pumpkin mash (see page 72) or canned pumpkin

What you do:

1 Preheat the oven to 425°F (220°C). Butter an 8-inch (20-cm) square pan.

2 Mix the flour, cornmeal, baking powder, and salt in a large bowl.

3 Whisk the egg, milk, and honey in a separate bowl. Whisk in the melted butter; add the pumpkin mash. Pour over the dry ingredients and stir, but do not beat.

4 Spread the batter into the pan. Bake for 20 to 25 minutes. Cut into squares.

Serves 6 to 8 kids a slice of warm cornbread.

The Pumpkin Seed's Story

Time for a change, pumpkin! You'll be baked and eaten, or carved and decorated. Get ready for some action!

Share Your Harvest

Many Native Americans believe that the food from the earth is meant for all people, so they share their garden harvest with others. You and your friends can continue that tradition by setting aside a portion of your pumpkin and (other garden vegetable) harvest for sharing with people at a local food shelf or homeless shelter. Add some homemade pumpkin foods, such as Pumpkin Cornbread, along with the fresh garden harvest, and perhaps a jug of apple cider. Slip in a bag of toasted pumpkin seeds for a treat! Have a grown-up help you deliver your harvest offering.

Ask your pumpkin what it wants to be.
A castle? A camel? A car?
Imagine the answer,
Then carve it or paint it.

Decorate a Pumpkin!

Put down plenty of newspaper as you begin. Then, let your imagination run wild!

COOKIE CUTTER SOLAR SYSTEM: Collect cookie cutters in the shapes of stars and moons. Trace them on all sides of the pumpkin with a washable marker. Then, cut out the shapes with a pumpkin carving tool (see Pumpkin Carving Tips, page 63).

ANIMAL ANTICS: Instead of cutting out the pumpkin, use paint or markers to draw faces of different animals on your pumpkins. Choose a theme, such as wild animals or endangered animals or pets. After you display your animal zoo, you can use the pumpkins for cooking.

NATURE KID: Decorate a pumpkin with nature finds. Collect twigs for hair and a corncob or pine cone for a nose. For additional features, gather gourds, cloves, corn kernels, and dried berries. Attach them to the pumpkin head with toothpicks. Stick twigs and cloves directly into the pumpkin.

PUMPKIN CARVING TIPS

◎ Always carve pumpkins with the help of a grown-up.

◎ Draw your design on the pumpkin with a washable marker.

◎ Use a store-bought pumpkin-carving tool, available at pharmacies and party supply stores.

◎ For best results, move the pumpkin cutter slowly with a steady, sawing motion.

◎ Carve away from yourself!

◎ Cut small features, such as eyes, first. Then, cut the nose and larger features.

◎ Scoop out seeds and slimy flesh with an ice cream scoop. Save them for eating or for next year's pumpkin garden.

TOTEM POLE: Stack four or more painted pumpkins on top of each other to make a totem pole. If they don't stand upright on their own, ask a grown-up to help you stake them together with a garden stake or branch. If you like, you can paint or carve the outer skin of the pumpkins with designs of nature, such as the sun, moon, birds, or animals, before you make the totem.

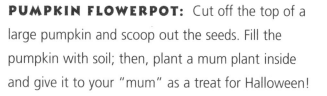

PUMPKIN FLOWERPOT: Cut off the top of a large pumpkin and scoop out the seeds. Fill the pumpkin with soil; then, plant a mum plant inside and give it to your "mum" as a treat for Halloween!

CREEPY CATERPILLAR: Remove the stems on 5 to 10 smallish pumpkins. Arrange them in a curving row on your lawn or porch. Poke sticks into the bottom of each one to make creepy crawly legs, and don't forget to paint or carve the face!

SAY SOMETHING! Cut the letters B, O, and O, and an exclamation point on four small pumpkins with a pumpkin-carving tool. Or fashion the words "Fall" or "Autumn" and use them as a decoration throughout the season. Illuminate your pumpkins with candles and set them out on your front porch.

In the Pumpkin Journal . . .

Tell or write a riddle about what grows in a garden, telling all about a pumpkin but not giving the name. You could begin by saying, "It's orange and round and good to eat." Add other descriptions. Tell your riddle to a friend and see if he or she can guess what you're describing.

Pumpkin Pun Fun!

How do you fix a broken jack-o'-lantern?

With a pumpkin patch!

What do you call a fat jack-o'-lantern?

A plumpkin!

PUMPKIN PONDERINGS

WHAT'S INSIDE?

Take a close look at what is going on inside the pumpkin as you carve it.

▼ How does the size of the pumpkin relate to the size of the seed? It makes sense, doesn't it: Bigger seeds for bigger pumpkins.

▼ Do all pumpkins have the same number of seeds? Rinse the goo off the seeds, then count them by 2s, 3s, 4s, or 5s to help you keep the numbers straight.

▼ How thick is the skin of a pumpkin? Use a ruler to help you decide. How thick is the flesh inside? If you grew more than one type of pumpkin, compare how the two types look inside and out.

Popcorn Jack

Make some of these orange popcorn balls with a friend as a homemade trick-or-treat offering.

What you need:

- ½ cup (125 ml) butter or margarine
- 2 10-ounce (289 g) packages marshmallows
- Orange food coloring paste (available at party supply stores)
- 15 cups (3.75 liters) popped popcorn
- Chocolate chips, M&Ms, fruit leather, or other candies
- Black licorice

What you do:

1 Melt the butter in a nonstick saucepan over medium heat. Add the marshmallows, and stir until melted. Add a few dabs of the food coloring paste.

2 Pour the popcorn into a large mixing bowl. Pour the melted marshmallows over the popcorn and stir to coat (this will be sticky).

3 Grease your clean hands with a dab of butter or margarine; then, form the popcorn into balls.

4 At the top of each popcorn ball, add a stem: a short piece of black licorice. For a jack-o'-lantern popcorn ball, press chocolate chips, M&Ms, or other candies onto the face of the popcorn ball for eyes, a mouth, and a nose.

Pumpkin Lore

J A C K   W H O ?

Ever wonder how the jack-o'-lantern got its name? According to one Irish folktale, a man named Jack was so mischievous, he was ordered to walk the earth until Judgment Day. To light his way, he carried a lantern carved from a turnip!

Or, cut the features out of fruit leather with clean scissors. Wrap the pumpkins in plastic wrap and tie with a green ribbon. The pumpkins can be stored for up to a week. Enjoy!

Makes 15 to 20 pumpkin-shaped treats.

Pumpkin Lore

HALLOWEEN HAPPENINGS LONG AGO

Ever wonder why we carve pumpkins, dress in costume, and go house to house on Halloween? Our modern-day traditions have their roots in ancient Irish history. In those days, the Celtic festival of Samhain (or summer's end) was celebrated on October 31, the last day of autumn before the cold of winter. People believed that on that dark, long night, the spirits of friends, family, or foes might come back to visit. To welcome friendly souls and chase away any evil spirits, the Celtic people dressed in animal skins and lit huge bonfires. Irish children who had to walk the roads in the evening darkness carried lanterns carved out of turnips and lit with burning embers of peat. As they went along their way, they begged for more embers at each house they came to . . . just as we go trick-or-treating today!

When the Irish immigrants came to America in the 1840s, they brought along their customs from what they then called All Hallows' Eve. Though they didn't find many turnips in the new land, they found plenty of pumpkins. So nowadays, we carve our jack-o-lanterns out of pumpkins!

In the Pumpkin Journal . . .

Pretend that you are living during that time so long ago. It's the last day of autumn, and the days are getting shorter. There is no electricity or running water, just fires in the family hearth. Instead of using wood for fires, you use peat, harvested from the fields. It is dark as you and your friends walk home. Thank goodness you have your turnip lanterns! As you make your journey, you go from house to house, asking neighbors for peat embers to light your way. The light of the lantern is dim. It flickers in the wind. What are you thinking as you make the journey? Use a pencil to sketch and shade what you see as you walk along in the dark with your turnip lantern. Write a caption to describe it.

The pumpkin is wearing
A fanciful face.
Now tend to the seeds
Before they get out of place!

Tasty Toasted Pumpkin Seeds

Don't discard your pumpkin seeds when you carve your pumpkin! Toast them for a healthy snack or salad topping.

What you need:

1 small pumpkin
2 tablespoons (25 ml) vegetable oil
Salt

What you do:

1 Have a grown-up cut the pumpkin in half. Scoop the seeds out into a large bowl.

2 Now for the tough part: Separate the seeds from the pumpkin fiber. Do this messy job outside if it's warm enough, or in the kitchen with lots of newspaper. There's no trick to it, except for soaking the seeds in water, so just enjoy the slimy feeling! Have a bowl of fresh water nearby, and a colander, too.

3 Place the rinsed pumpkin seeds in a bowl, drizzle with the oil, and sprinkle with salt. Toss well.

4 Preheat the oven to 300°F (149°C). Spread the seeds out on a cookie sheet. Bake for 30 to 40 minutes, or until slightly brown and crisp.

Makes about 2 cups (500 ml) of a nutty harvest snack.

Kids' Pumpkin Projects

Pumpkin Trail Mix

Northeastern Native Americans snacked on raw pumpkin seeds and cranberries sweetened with maple syrup. This trail mix combines these flavors in a crunchy snack that will give you energy on the hiking trail this fall.

What you need:

2 cups (500 ml) raw sunflower seeds
2 cups (500 ml) pumpkin seeds
1 cup (250 ml) raisins
1 cup (250 ml) sweetened dried cranberries

What you do:

Measure the ingredients into a paper bag, fold over the top of the bag, and shake to mix. Store the mixture in an airtight plastic bag or container.

Makes 1 cup (250 ml) each for 6 stalwart hikers.

Craft a Pumpkin Seed Necklace

String the seeds of your pumpkin into a pretty necklace. Use fresh seeds, not dry ones. Wear it yourself, give it as a gift, or hang it around your scarecrow's neck for an autumn decoration.

What you need:

Fresh pumpkin seeds ◆ Paper towels ◆ Sewing needle ◆ Waxed dental floss ◆ A sewing needle ◆ Cardboard

What you do:

1 Remove any pumpkin pulp from the seeds. Rinse the seeds with water; then, pat them dry with paper towels.

2 Ask a grown-up to help you thread the sewing needle with a piece of waxed dental floss. When tied into a loop, the floss should be long enough to slip over your head.

3 Push the needle through one seed and pull until the floss is a few inches from the end of the seed. Knot the end of the floss.

4 String on more seeds until the floss is full. If you have trouble stringing the seeds, place them, one at a time, on top of a piece of cardboard and poke the needle through the seed. Then, tie the ends of the floss together. The necklace is ready to wear!

COLORED SEED NECKLACE: In a saucepan, mix together a few drops of food coloring and 1 cup (250 ml) of water. Ask a grown-up to boil the mixture for 5 minutes. Soak the seeds in the mixture until they look a little darker than you want them to. Rinse the seeds under cold water and spread them out on cardboard to air dry. String the dried seeds into a colorful necklace.

What will you make
With your pumpkin?
Do the Pumpkin Mash
And feast like a Pilgrim!

Do the Pumpkin Mash!

Use this bright orange squashed pumpkin meat to bake bread, muffins, cookies, or pies.

What you need:

1 medium-sized pie pumpkin, such as Sugar

What you do:

1   Cut the pumpkin in half (ask a grown-up for help). Place it on a cookie sheet, cut-side up, and prick the skin with a fork.

2   Preheat the oven to 375°F (190°C) and bake for 50 minutes, or until it is very soft when poked with a fork.

3   Let the pumpkin cool. Scoop out the seeds with a big spoon. Scoop out the pumpkin flesh. Put the skin in your compost pile. Mash the pumpkin flesh with a potato masher or puree in a food processor with the help of a grown-up.

FROZEN PUMPKIN MASH: If you have more pumpkin mash then you know what to do with, pop the cooled mash in a plastic container, leaving about 1 inch (2.5 cm) at the top. Put a tight-fitting lid on it and freeze. On a chilly winter's day, you can defrost the pumpkin mash and bake yourself a pie!

PUMPKINS GET AN A+

Pumpkins have a glowing complexion — and so will you if you eat one! Pumpkins are loaded with vitamin A, which gives you smooth skin, strong teeth, and good vision. What other foods are high in vitamin A? If you're thinking of dark green or orange ones, like carrots, sweet potatoes, broccoli, spinach, and cantaloupe, you already know a lot about good nutrition! Pumpkin flesh (that's what the inside of the pumpkin is called) is also low in calories and it packs in some vitamin B and C, too. In fact, eating pumpkins might even help reduce your chances of catching a cold!

Three Sisters Succotash

One of the best ways to get the "glow" vitamins and minerals from the pumpkin is to steam it in a succotash, using all of the crops from your Native American Three Sisters garden. In a saucepan filled with a few inches of water, steam corn kernels (fresh, frozen, or canned), lima or string beans, and cubed squash or pumpkin until soft. Season with salt and pepper and serve with melted butter.

SUCCOTASH WITH A DASH: Add red pepper and onion, cut into small pieces and cooked in butter until soft, for a colorful, delicious accent.

THREE SISTERS SUCCOTASH BURRITO: Spoon the succotash into a flour tortilla and top with grated cheese and salsa. Roll up the tortilla and warm the burrito in a toaster oven at 350°F (180°C) for 5 to 7 minutes, or microwave on high for 1 minute until the cheese melts.

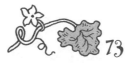

Pumpkin Lore

At Thanksgiving, we hear the story of the Pilgrims, who sailed from Europe on the Mayflower to settle in America. When they landed on Cape Cod on November 10, 1620, it was too late in the year to plant the wheat and rye seeds they had brought with them. Without food, more than half of the Pilgrims died in that first cold New England winter. Here is a retelling of a tale about a Native American who made a big difference.

THE GIFT FROM SQUANTO

Imagine that you are one of the Pilgrim children who traveled across the Atlantic on the Mayflower. During the first cold winter in America, you spend your days stoking the fire and huddling nearby with your family to keep warm. You have very little to eat, just a few acorns and a little soup, but not enough food to fill your stomach. Each day, it feels colder outside. And more and more of your friends grow weak and sick. It seems as if the winter will never end.

But finally, it is spring. The snow begins to melt and the first green sprouts appear in the field and in the forest. When the weather warms up, you help your parents plant the rye and wheat seeds that you brought with you. The weather grows warmer, and you wait patiently for the seeds to grow. But something is wrong—the seeds never sprout!

Just when you give up hope, a Native American man appears in the field. His name is Tisquantum, or Squanto. Unlike the other Native Americans you have met, he speaks your language. He says, "Friends, I

can see that you are hungry. I have come to teach you how to grow food in this land."

Squanto has brought you and the other Pilgrims a basket of seed corn. Corn, he says, grows well in this new home. He shows you how to plant the seeds in hills. He places three fish in the ground for fertilizer and covers it with a mound of soil. All summer long, Squanto helps you tend the crops. He also teaches you how to catch eels, hunt wild turkey, and forage for wild foods.

In the autumn, the Pilgrim harvest is bountiful, thanks to Squanto's help. To celebrate, you and the other settlers decide to host a big feast. You invite Squanto and his Native American friends to come enjoy your food. You dine on fresh vegetables, meats, fish, and delicious fruits. The feast—now remembered and celebrated as Thanksgiving—lasts for three days!

Now get ready to make pie,
Lots of melt-in-your-mouth
Pumpkin pie.
Eat it all up!

Best-Ever Pumpkin Pie!

Have you ever made pumpkin pie from a real pumpkin? Many people buy canned pumpkin, but wait until you taste a bite of fresh pumpkin pie. You'll shout, "Save room for pie!"

What you need:

3 eggs

½ cup (125 ml) sugar

¼ cup (50 ml) brown sugar

2 cups (500 ml) pumpkin mash (see recipe on page 72)

1 teaspoon (5 ml) cinnamon

¼ teaspoon (1 ml) ginger

¼ teaspoon (1 ml) cloves

¼ teaspoon (1 ml) salt

1 12-ounce (375 ml) can evaporated milk

1 unbaked piecrust

What you do:

1 Preheat the oven to 450°F (230°C). In a large mixing bowl, beat the eggs and sugars. Blend in the pumpkin mash, the spices, salt, and evaporated milk.

2 Pour the filling into the piecrust.

3 Bake at 450°F (230°C) for 10 minutes; then, reduce the heat to 350°F (180°C) and bake for another 50 minutes, or until the pie sets. Cool, then slice.

Serves 6 to 8 kids a slice of real pumpkin pie!

MINI-PUMPKIN PIES: Pour the filling into mini-pie shells (available at most grocery stores) and bake according to pie shell directions.

PILGRIM PUMPKIN PIE

The Pilgrims didn't always bake their pumpkin pie in a pie shell. They baked it in a pumpkin shell! They cut off the top and scooped out all the seeds. Next, they filled it with milk, sugar, spices, and sliced apples. The top went back on and the whole pumpkin was roasted in the ashes of the fire.

PUMPKIN PONDERINGS

PUMPKIN PIE MATH

In your pumpkin journal, draw three different pies. Pretend you have to serve eight people. Divide the first pie into eight pieces using four lines. Using two lines, cut another pie into four pieces to serve four people. Now you're ready to cut a real pie into a portion for each person in your family. How many pieces will you need to cut? What fraction, or part, of the pie will each person in your family eat?

DIGGING DEEPER... Pilgrim Table Manners

Before a meal, the Pilgrims would tie big napkins that hung all the way down to their knees, around their necks. They used these napkins to wipe their hands and to pick up hot foods, and they scooped their food with seashell spoons! The Pilgrims ate pumpkins everyday: pumpkin bread, pumpkin pie, and even pumpkin-seed cereal for breakfast! Sometimes they dried the pumpkin shell and used it as a bowl or a dish.

THE PILGRIM'S PUMPKIN

We have pumpkin at morning

And pumpkin at noon;

If it was not for pumpkin,

We would be undoon.

—OLD PILGRIM RHYME

WINTER

Bedtime for the Pumpkin Patch, Saving Seeds, and Pumpkin Tales, Food, and Crafts

You've tended your pumpkin garden and decorated the big, round globes. You've celebrated the harvest with stories and games, and you've tasted fresh pumpkin baked into cookies, muffins, pie, and cornbread. Now you and your pumpkin patch deserve a rest.

Winter is a quiet time in the garden. Store your pumpkins and put the pumpkin patch to bed. Then head indoors for some winter fun! Keep the spirit of the pumpkin garden alive over the winter by saving seeds from this year's pumpkins to plant next spring. Eat pumpkin pancakes and pumpkin soup while you make pumpkin candles and pumpkin seed soap. Have a pumpkin tea party. Pull up an armchair and get cozy with a pumpkin tale. Or tell your own pumpkin story!

As autumn leaves wither,
Bring your pumpkins indoors
To store for winter,
And put the garden to bed.

"Winterize" Your Pumpkins

Native Americans and Pilgrims feasted on pumpkins throughout the winter. For fresh pumpkin pie all winter long, follow these steps to keep your pumpkin harvest in tip-top shape.

What you need:

Pumpkins ✦ Hay bale or slatted shelf ✦ Dry basement or unheated attic that won't freeze ✦ Indoor thermometer ✦ Cloth for wiping pumpkins

What you do:

1 Choose fresh, unblemished pumpkins. Make sure their shells are hard and the stems are still attached.

2 Set the pumpkins in a warm (75°F to 80°F; 24°C to 27°C), dry place for a week or so to "cure."

3 Find a cool, dry place to store your pumpkins. A dry basement or an unheated attic are two good choices. Check the temperature with the thermometer. It should be between 50°F (10°C) and 60°F (16°C). Be sure the space won't freeze.

4 Place the pumpkins on the slatted shelf or hay bale to allow the air to circulate around them. Keep your pumpkins apart—no touching!

5 Check your pumpkins every week. If you see mold on the shells, wipe them clean with a dry cloth.

6 Enjoy your fresh pumpkins all winter long!

Enjoy a Pumpkin Tea Party!

In the book *Little House in the Big Woods* by Laura Ingalls Wilder, Mary and Laura have a pumpkin tea party in the attic, using a big pumpkin for a table and little pumpkins for chairs. Pretend you are one of the characters in the story. Bring out a tea set and find a special place to have your tea. Add a mini-pumpkin centerpiece. Enjoy a pumpkin tea party of your own!

Pumpkin Lore

STORING PUMPKINS LONG AGO

The Iroquois Indians of New York and Canada piled pumpkins into a bark-lined underground pit to store for the winter. The Menomini Indians of Wisconsin cut the pumpkins into strips that they dried and braided together.

Put Your Pumpkin Patch to Bed!

You made your pumpkin bed in the spring. Now it's time to make it again for the long, cold winter! When should your pumpkin patch go to bed? Take a look around your garden in the late summer and fall to help you decide. Is the soil getting frosty? Does it get rainy this time of year? You want to put the garden to bed before the soil gets too wet or cold to work.

What you need:

A digging fork or shovel ◆ Aged manure (available at garden supply stores) or compost
◆ Mulch (old leaves and grass clippings)

What you do:

1 As your pumpkins are picked, pull up any roots, vines, weeds, or rotten pumpkins in your garden plot and put them in a compost pile.

2 Next, ask a grown-up to help you dig into the soil to loosen it up. Dig at least 1 foot (30 cm) deep and break up all the clumps and lumps.

3 Pumpkins eat a lot as they grow. To help replace the "groceries" in the soil, add a couple of inches of compost or aged manure all over your pumpkin plot. Mix it in with your shovel; then, smooth it out.

4 Fed and covered with mulch, your pumpkin bed will stay cozy all winter long! And next spring, preparing your pumpkin bed will be a snap.

Hearty, Hot, Homemade Pumpkin Soup

*A*fter you've made your pumpkin bed for winter, cook up a cold-weather lunch or supper. Roast a pumpkin to use in this soup that was a favorite among the Iroquois Indians of New York and Canada.

What you need:

1 medium-sized pumpkin
4 cups (1 liter) chicken broth
¼ cup (50 ml) maple syrup
1 tablespoon (15 ml) butter or margarine
½ teaspoon (2 ml) cinnamon
½ teaspoon (2 ml) nutmeg
½ teaspoon (2 ml) salt

What you do:

1 Preheat the oven to 350°F (180°C). Ask a grown-up to help you slice the pumpkin in half and scoop out the seeds. Place the halves cut-side down on a buttered cookie sheet. Bake for 1 hour.

2 Use a big metal spoon to scoop out the pumpkin flesh. Then, mash the flesh with a potato masher.

3 In a heavy saucepan, combine the pumpkin with the rest of the ingredients. Warm over low heat, stirring occasionally.

Serves 6 to 8 kids a hot, hearty meal.

SOUP IN A PUMPKIN SHELL: Hollow out a pumpkin and use it as a soup serving bowl!

SIMPLE SQUASH SOUP: Other winter squashes can be used in place of the pumpkin. (But then it won't be *pumpkin* soup!)

Reach into a fresh-cut pumpkin,
Take out a gooey glob of seeds,
Pick some, rinse, and dry them,
And save for next year's pumpkin plot.

Be a Pumpkin-Seed Saver!

Keep the spirit of this year's pumpkin garden going by saving some seeds to plant next spring. By saving seeds, you become part of a tradition that has been going on for thousands of years! When you plant them, you'll be growing a bit of history right in your own backyard. Awesome, isn't it?

What you need:

A pumpkin you like ◆ Water ◆ Colander ◆ Window screen ◆ Baby food jar or small mayonnaise jar ◆ Sticker label ◆ Marker

What you do:

1 Have a grown-up help you cut open the pumpkin and remove the seeds. Separate the seeds from the pulp with your fingers as much as possible. Place the seeds in a colander and rinse under cold water to remove any extra fiber.

2 Spread the clean seeds in a single layer on a window screen, cookie sheets, or ceramic dish to air-dry out of direct sunlight for several days or even a week. Turn the seeds several times during the day to be sure they dry completely.

3 Once the seeds are thoroughly dry, place them in a jar with a sealable lid.

4 To keep track of your seeds, write the date you save them and the name of the pumpkin variety on a sticker and attach it to the jar.

5 Store the seeds in a dry, dark, cool spot (the back of a cupboard is ideal).

6 Next spring, plant your pumpkin seeds, and share your seed supply with others!

The Pumpkin Seed's Story

The pumpkin seed has grown to seedling, plant, and fruit. Now the pumpkin waits to pass on its gift of seeds for growing *next* summer's pumpkins!

DIGGING DEEPER...

Tradition!

Thanks to seed savers, seeds available today might be a variety grown by your ancestors, or by the native people of other areas. If you want to grow an old-fashioned vegetable such as Seminole pumpkin, grown in Florida by the Seminole Indians in the 1500s, for example, you can order the seed from **Southern Exposure Seed Exchange**, P.O. Box 170, Earlysville, VA 22936. Or try Amish Pie pumpkin, an heirloom from the Maryland mountains, available from the **Seed Savers' Exchange** (a nonprofit seed-saving group based at 3076 North Winn Rd., Decorah, IA 52101). Another good source of heirloom seed from the Southwest is **Native Seeds/ Search** at 2509 North Campbell Ave., #325, Tucson, AZ 85719. To correspond or swap seeds with other gardeners or groups who are collecting seed, check out the **National Gardening Association** website at *www.garden.org,* or try *http://homearts. com/helpers/swap/main/swapc1.htm.*

Make a Hopi Seed Pot

In traditional Native American times, being the seed carrier was felt to be a great privilege, because the seed carrier held the next year's harvest. To protect their precious seeds all winter, the women of the Hopi Indian nation of the Southwest made pots out of coils of clay. Here's how to store your saved pumpkin seeds Hopi-Indian style.

What you need:

Air-dry clay ◆ Water ◆ Tempera paints ◆
Paintbrush ◆ Dried pumpkin seeds

What you do:

1 Shape a fist-sized piece of clay into a shallow bowl. This will be the base of your pot.

2 Roll another piece of clay between your palms to make a coil that will fit along the top of the shallow bowl. The coil should be about ¾ inch (2 cm) in diameter.

3 Lay the coil around the rim of the bowl, pinching it in place as you go. Add more coils to the pot in the same way until the pot is as high as you like it.

4 Dampen your fingers with water; then, smooth over the joints between the coils.

5 Let the pot air-dry; then, decorate it with tempera paints. Once the paint dries, fill it with dried pumpkin seeds and store them in a cool, dry place until next spring.

PUMPKIN PONDERINGS

SEED FOR THOUGHT

▼ Pumpkin seeds that have been stored in a cool, dry, dark spot in an airtight container can stay good for planting for up to six years. That's some sturdy seed!

▼ If you grow more than one variety of pumpkin or squash in your garden, the pollen on the plants might "cross." Be prepared to get a surprise when you plant seed saved from crossed pumpkins — you may end up with a pump-zuke!

In the Pumpkin Journal . . .

Have you read the story *Miss Rumphius* by Barbara Cooney? In the book, Miss Rumphius is a seed saver and seed carrier of lupine flower seeds. Have someone read you the story or read it yourself. Would you like to be like Miss Rumphius? Imagine that you could plant whatever you wanted to make the world a better place. What would it be? Use water-colors to paint a picture of what you imagine. Date your picture and write a caption.

The seeds are safely sheltered
And the garden's tucked in bed.
Come inside for winter fun and food,
and crafts from way back when.

Pumpkin Seed Soap

*I*n colonial times, winter was spent making clothes and household items such as soap, mending tools, and keeping warm by the fire. On a blustery winter day, turn a few pumpkin seeds into soap for scrubbing your garden hands next spring. Give an extra bar to a gardening friend!

What you need:

1 4-ounce (100 g) bar of glycerin soap (available at health food stores) ◆ 2 tablespoons (25 ml) coarsely chopped pumpkin seeds ◆ Empty coffee can ◆ Muffin tin and liners or cookie or candy molds with aluminum foil

What you do:

1 Place the soap in a coffee can and set it in a saucepan of water.

2 With the help of a grown-up, bring the water to a gentle boil. Continue boiling until the soap melts.

3 Stir in the pumpkin seeds. Using a pot holder, remove the coffee can from the water. Then, ask a grown-up to carefully pour the melted soap into a muffin tin lined with foil liners or other molds covered with aluminum foil.

4 Once hardened, the pumpkin soap is ready for scrubbing!

Makes 4 mini-bars of garden soap.

Craft a Pumpkin Candle Holder

*L*ight up a cool, dark night with these bright lights.

What you need:

Mini-pumpkins ✦ 1 candle for each
pumpkin ✦ Sharp knife

What you do:

1 Ask a grown-up to help you carve out a hole in the top of a mini-pumpkin. Make sure the hole is no bigger than a quarter.

2 Remove the seeds with a small spoon or the tip of an apple corer.

3 Stick a candle into the hole. Then, ask a grown-up to light it at the dinner table!

DIGGING DEEPER . . . Make a Homemade Gift Basket

*I*n the Native American tradition of caring for others around us, especially our elders, fill a gift basket to give to a shut-in or other senior member of your neighborhood. Ask a grown-up to help you with the cooking and collecting. Your gift might include Pumpkin Muffins or Pumpkin Cookies, fresh fruit, a decorated painted mini-pumpkin or a Pumpkin Candle Holder with candles, and a brightly wrapped package of Pumpkin Seed Soap. Craft a cheery pumpkin card out of construction paper to go with your gift.

Pumpkin Pancakes!

$\mathcal{S}$erve these orange hotcakes with warm maple syrup on a cold winter morning.

What you need:

2 cups (500 ml) flour

1 tablespoon (15 ml) baking powder

½ teaspoon (2 ml) salt

2 tablespoons (25 ml) sugar

1 teaspoon (5 ml) pumpkin pie spice

2 eggs

1¾ cups (425 ml) milk

3 tablespoons (40 ml) oil or melted butter, plus 1 tablespoon (15 ml) for frying

½ cup (125 ml) pumpkin mash (see page 72)

What you do:

1 Sift the flour, baking powder, salt, sugar, and pumpkin pie spice in a large bowl.

2 Whisk the eggs and milk in a separate bowl. Whisk in the butter or oil and the pumpkin mash. Pour over the dry ingredients and stir, but do not beat. It's okay if the batter is lumpy.

3 Melt 1 tablespoon (15 ml) butter in a griddle or an electric skillet over medium high. Then, being careful not to splatter the hot butter, drop about ¼ cup (50 ml) of batter for each regular-sized pancake. Be sure to leave enough room between the cakes for them to grow. Drizzle the batter into a pumpkin shape!

4 Cook until the pancakes bubble on the top and brown on the bottom. Flip; then, cook until brown on other side.

Makes 20 pancakes, enough to serve 5 hungry kids a hearty breakfast.

PUMPKIN WAFFLES: To make waffles, follow the same recipe, but separate the eggs. Combine the yolks with the milk, 3 tablespoons (40 ml) of oil or butter, and pumpkin mash. Stir into the dry ingredients. Beat the egg whites until stiff and gently fold into the batter. Cook on a greased waffle iron until lightly browned.

Finish your pumpkin journal
With pages you've tended all year,
And as winter winds howl,
Harvest pumpkin stories and tales.

A Season for Storytelling

$\mathcal{S}$tories are like gardens. When you tell one, you give it life and help it grow. This winter, grow some stories with your friends and family members. For inspiration, use a storytelling bag.

What you need:

A pillowcase or paper bag ◆ A small pumpkin or a drawing of a pumpkin ◆ Household and nature finds, such as a feather, pinecone, picture of a sun, water (in a jar), pencil, or a piece of clothing

What you do:

1. Gather round in a circle with as many people as you like. Sit down so everyone is comfortable. Put all the props into the pillowcase or bag.

2. The first person should reach into the bag and begin the story, working the prop he or she picked into the tale. For instance, say the first person picked the pumpkin. He might begin the story by saying, "Once there was a great pumpkin that was filled with magical water."

3. The next person should reach into the bag, pick a prop, and work her prop into the story.

4. Continue going around the circle, picking props from the storytelling bag, and telling the story until you feel it's complete.

5. If you'd like, you can record the story on tape. When you're finished, write it down in a book and illustrate the story with drawings.

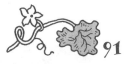

Pumpkin Lore

NATIVE AMERICAN STORYTELLING

The Northeastern Native Americans, such as the Wampanoag Indians, who lived in the Cape Cod area, or the Iroquois, who lived in New York and Canada, would tell stories during the winter, between the first and last frosts of the year. Some believed that if the crops heard their stories during the summer months, they wouldn't grow because they would think it was winter.

DIGGING DEEPER...

Pumpkin Tales

Pumpkins show up in many legends, myths, and fairy tales. The magical pumpkin is often filled with a treasure, such as water, fish, precious oil, silver, gold, or even a year's supply of rice. Head to the local library and look for stories that star pumpkins. Learn the story, then retell it to your friend. Here's one to get you going.

PRINCESS SCARGO'S BIRTHDAY PUMPKIN

Long ago in the narrow land that is now known as Cape Cod, there was a child born — the only daughter of the great Chief Sagum. Her father named her Princess Scargo, which meant "new life." As the princess grew, she became more and more fond of the creatures of the forest. She took care of them — and they returned her affection. She also loved the creatures who swam in the liquid heaven of water. It was her secret wish to someday love and care for them the same way she loved and cared for the creatures of the land.

It was a custom that the children of chiefs would receive birthday presents from the chiefs of neighboring tribes, and on her seventh birthday, Princess Scargo received many marvelous gifts. One chief brought her a deer carved from a block of wood; another chief gave her a basket of hollow robin's eggs. But the best present of all was a giant pumpkin, one that took many days to transport it across the land. When it arrived, the entire tribe stood and stared at it. Carved on the gleaming orange side of the giant pumpkin were pictures of the Princess's friends of the land — the fox, the wolf, and other creatures. Inside, lived miniature creatures of the water: tiny swimming fish of many colors. Princess Scargo cherished the pumpkin and its inhabitants.

That spring, the rains never came. The streams and ponds began to dry up and many fish died. The people worried because they relied on fish for food. So Chief Sagum called a council. It was decided that everyone in the tribe would help to dig a pond that was large enough and deep enough to withstand the longest drought.

The people of the tribe got to work. Princess Scargo wanted to help, too. But the men of the tribe said she was too small to dig. She asked the oldest squaws if she could help them make baskets to carry the sand, but they said that daughters of chiefs are not allowed to weave baskets. Princess Scargo longed to do something to help.

When the heavens opened and the long-awaited rain poured forth, the people rejoiced. Day by day the great hole filled with more water. But it would take many years to replenish the supply of fish. Chief Sagum assured them that there was nothing more they could do. "We have given of ourselves. That is all that we can give."

Princess Scargo heard her father's words. Yet, she hadn't given of herself; her job was not done. She stared into her great pumpkin—and suddenly she had a wonderful idea. In her most tender voice, she spoke to the fish that inhabited her great pumpkin and told them of their new home to be. She promised to visit them every day.

The next day, the people of the tribe noticed a very strange thing. The pond was very quickly, quite mysteriously, and seemingly impossibly filled with fish! To this day, as the legend goes, the great-great-great-great-grandfish of Princess Scargo's fish still swim in Scargo Lake. And if you stand at the top of the nearby hill and look down at the shimmering water, you'll notice that the lake is shaped like a giant fish.

WINTER

The seeds are saved, the crafts are made,
The pumpkin patch is sleeping.
It's time for pumpkin dreams
Until the cycle starts again!

"Plant" a Play Clay Pumpkin Patch

On a cold winter day, make a pumpkin patch out of play clay.

What you'll need:

1 cup (250 ml) all-purpose flour
1 cup (250 ml) water
½ cup (125 ml) salt
1 teaspoon (5 ml) vegetable oil
½ teaspoon (2 ml) cream of tartar
Orange and green food coloring paste
Waxed paper

What you do:

1 With the help of a grown-up, mix the flour, water, salt, oil, and cream of tartar in a saucepan. Cook over medium heat until the mixture holds together (keep mixing, or the dough will stick to the bottom of the pan).

2 When the play dough is cool enough to touch, divide it in half. Knead a dab of orange food coloring paste into one half and a dab of green food coloring paste into the other half (use a toothpick to do this so you don't add too much food coloring).

3   Working over a sheet of waxed paper, roll the orange play dough into pumpkins. You can make mini clay pumpkins, like the Jack Be Little, or giant ones like Big Max or Atlantic Giant.

4   Connect them with a rambling vine made out of green clay. Add a bunch of leaves, cut with a plastic knife out of rolled-out green dough, and your pumpkin patch is complete. Display it on a kitchen tray or a piece of cardboard covered with aluminum foil. For even more fun, create an entire vegetable garden out of clay.

The Pumpkin Seed's Story

Your pumpkin journal has gone through all four seasons: spring, summer, fall, and winter. Its pages are brimming with your pumpkin tale. Who would have thought that some tiny pumpkin seeds could make a book so full? The story of the pumpkin seed has come to a stopping point, for now. But although this year's pumpkin journey is coming to an end, the next pumpkin season is right around the corner. Another pumpkin seed is waiting to be planted, watered, weeded, and tended with care, and celebrated in the garden. A pumpkin-to-be is waiting to be decorated and cooked into muffins, and cornbread, and pie. Another harvest hoe-down is waiting to be planned. Get ready!

Resources

A Native American Feast by Lucille Recht Penner (Simon & Schuster, 1994). Recipes from Native North Americans.

Native American Gardening by Michael J. Caduto and Joseph Bruchac (Fulcrum Publishing, 1996). Native American harvest and planting tales, family gardening activities, and recipes.

In the Three Sisters Garden by JoAnne Dennee with Jack Peduzzi and Julia Hand (Kendall Hunt, 1995). A resource for kids to delve deeper into Native American gardening in an earth-friendly manner, with hands-on activities, stories, and recipes. Available from Food Works, 64 Main St., Montpelier, VT 05602; 802/223-1515.

The Perfect Pumpkin by Gail Damerow (Storey Publishing, 1997). Harvesting and growing techniques, recipes, and art and craft projects for the serious pumpkin grower.

The Pilgrims at Plymouth Rock by Lucille Recht Penner (Random House, 1996).

Squanto and the First Thanksgiving, narrated by Graham Greene with music by Paul McCandless (Rabbit Ears Productions, Inc., 1992).

Princess Scargo and the Birthday Pumpkin, narrated by Geena Davis with music by Michael Hedges (Rabbit Ears Productions, Inc., 1992).